AVOIDING MISTAKES IN YOUR SMALL BUSINESS

by David Karlson, Ph.D.

THE
CRISP
SMALL BUSINESS &
ENTREPRENEURSHIP
SERIES

CREDITS

Editor: Beverly Manber

Layout/Design: ExecuStaff

Cover Design: Kathleen Gadway

Library of Congress 92-54375
ISBN-1-56052-173-2

INTRODUCTION TO THE SERIES

This series of books is intended to inform and assist those of you who are in the beginning stages of starting a new small business venture or who are considering such an undertaking.

It is because you are confident of your abilities that you are taking this step. These books will provide additional information and support along the way.

Not every new business will succeed. The more information you have about budgeting, cash flow management, accounts receivable, and marketing and employee management, the better prepared you will be for the inevitable pitfalls.

A unique feature of the Crisp Small Business & Entrepreneurship Series is the personal involvement exercises, which give you many opportunities to apply immediately the concepts presented to your own business.

In each book in the series, these exercises take the form of "Your Turn," a checklist to confirm your understanding of the concept just presented and "Ask Yourself," a series of chapter-ending questions designed to evaluate your overall understanding or commitment.

In addition, numerous case studies are included, and each book is cross-referenced to others in the series and to other publications.

BOOKS IN THE SERIES

ACKNOWLEDGEMENTS

The real stars of this book are all those small business owners who willingly shared their stories with me so that others might learn from their mistakes. I thank them for their unselfish generosity.

Thanks also go to Mary Jane Shearer, Director of the Small Business Development Center at Prince George's College in Largo, Maryland, and to Janice Carmichael, Director of the Small Business Development Center at Montgomery College in Bethesda, Maryland, for helping me to identify the patterns of small business mistakes that are presented in this book. A special thanks goes to Dr. Joseph Shields, President of Carroll Community College in Westminster, Maryland, for his total commitment to my career. No matter what course I take, he is always in my corner.

And to my family, Claire, Matthew and Cinda, for being so patient while I spent my "spare" time writing and couldn't go to the park with them. And to my beloved parents, Mike and Gerry Karlson, who from the start encouraged me to do my best and taught me the importance of reaching out and helping others. And my brother, Mike, and my sister, Martha, who provide consistent sources of inspiration and love.

Finally, deep thanks to my colleague and friend, Tom Mierzwa. Tom responded heartily when I asked him to contribute his experience with conflict resolution, and wrote the Chapter 6, "Business Relationship Mistakes," which deals with conflict management. Tom's experiences with small, start-up businesses as well as larger, established organizations have shown that fostering conflict, failing to recognize it, and failing to resolve or prevent it are among the most costly mistakes a business can make.

CONTENTS

CONTENTS (continued)

CHAPTER ONE

INTRODUCTION TO AVOIDING MISTAKES

STRATEGIC MARKET-ING

Too often, entrepreneurs focus on running their businesses and not on getting the business. This is especially true for business owners in start-up companies, who often spend their energy, money and time gearing up to do business, and neglect to spend enough on finding out what it takes to get and keep customers. Of course, running the business is important, but without customers you cannot run a business for very long.

Businesses generate their sales income by figuring out what customers need and then by filling those needs—this is known as strategic marketing. The best result a business owner can hope for is satisfied customers. If you do not generate sufficient income from satisfied customers, you will not stay in business.

This book is written to help entrepreneurs succeed with their small businesses, and to share a unique view of strategic marketing that can help reduce the alarmingly high rate of small business failures.

I have assisted many types of organizations in their efforts to increase revenues. My clients have included small business, corporations, government agency, professional and trade associations, and very small businesses—"mom and pop" operations. Over the years, the problems and mistakes I have seen fall into clear patterns that obstruct many businesses' ability to generate income. Regardless of the type of organization, principals tend to make the same types of mistakes.

These are the patterns of behavior—the mistakes—that I have identified as relating directly to business failures. The case studies and lessons to be learned from them that are contained in this book highlight the patterns of mistakes, which fall into five categories that directly affect a business's bottom line:

▶ Marketing

▶ Personnel

▶ Management

- ► Finances
- ► Relationships

Throughout this book, you will read a wide variety of experiences of entrepreneurs who have learned by their own mistakes—sometimes with fatal consequences—what it takes to stay in business.

WHY LOOK AT OTHER PEOPLES' MISTAKES?

Calling on a modern interpretation of the ancient adage, "learn from your mistakes," this book is written so that you can learn from other people's mistakes.

This book takes a different approach from the standard business book that tells you "how to succeed." The premise of those books is that if you emulate a success story, you will be successful. In this book, you'll have a chance to look at business experiences in a wider context. You'll examine what contributes to business failures and learn how you can benefit from those experiences.

So the orientation here is geared around how *not to* do business!

WHY IS ONLY ONE OUT OF EVERY FIVE BUSINESSES SUCCESSFUL?

There seem to be a million reasons for a business to fail, evidenced by the great numbers of businesses that close their doors every day. Why is that? Are there really a million different ways to fail or do businesses make the same types of mistakes over and over?

I believe that there are very few reasons for businesses to fail. Instead, too many businesses are doomed when they repeat the same mistakes. And, in every failing situation there is at least one alternative that could have saved the business if the owner had known about it beforehand. Therefore, we can learn a lot about success by identifying the patterns that led to the failure and then avoiding those patterns.

By understanding the pitfalls of doing business, we have a chance to change the shocking statistics about business failure—especially for those who start up and fail within the first few years, when the numbers of failed businesses are the most dramatic. In each of the case studies in this book, you will look at a failure behavior to learn what success behavior(s) would have worked effectively in its place—what could or should have been done to do it right the first time.

CAN YOU AFFORD TO MAKE CLASSIC BUSINESS MISTAKES?

Few people, if any, have unlimited resources to invest in business ventures that are supposed to generate profits, but do not. Learning from your own mistakes is not a good idea unless you have resources to burn. Like most new business owners, your precious resources are probably scarce, and you have to get the most mileage out of them. By learning from the mistakes of others, you will have an opportunity to avoid the mistakes you know about. If you are lucky, you will make only a few new and creative mistakes of your own.

Seriously, most organizations—large and small, profit and nonprofit—have only a single chance to make it. Can you afford to risk not making it, just because you did not do your homework? After you answer the *Your Turn* and *Ask Yourself* exercises in each chapter, you will be in a good strategic position to avoid making the mistakes that could drain your business's success.

MAKING A MISTAKE VERSUS MISTAKE BEHAVIOR

The behaviors that I have observed are common in so many people that I call them "mistake behavior." People make the mistakes almost predictably. And when they do, their businesses always fail.

Business owners make other, isolated mistakes that have not been observed repeatedly or regularly, and which this book will not address. The patterns that you read about in this book are behaviors that you will want to avoid.

HOW BIG AND DEVASTATING ARE THESE MISTAKES?

One business person's small mistake can be another's catastrophic mistake. The impact of a mistake is different, depending on the individual circumstances of a business. With many variables at work in any given situation, the same mistake might have major impact on one business and another business might withstand it and just refer to it as "the close one that almost ruined us."

LEARNING FROM OTHERS' MISTAKES

Over and over, business owners have told me that they have learned their most important lessons from their bad decisions—from their mistakes. These people, whose businesses are not necessarily spectacularly successful, manage to pay their bills and stay in business. They represent standard business people, rather than exceptional, isolated "big success" stories. Their mistakes are the source of the case studies found in this book. Those who have been fortunate, got a second chance and did not make the same mistakes twice. Others were not so lucky; their businesses did not make it.

Many business owners don't get a second chance for what may seem like obvious reasons—principally, the lack of funds to carry on. When you dig deeper, you will see that the reasons are more specific than mere funds, and once you know the reasons—the mistakes—you can avoid them. Those business owners who share their close-call stories have provided wonderful, convincing insight into the mistakes that absolutely must be avoided if a business is going to be successful.

AFTER YOU READ THIS BOOK

When you finish this book you will be able to avoid the question, "How could I make such a stupid mistake?"

You will understand that some mistakes take a lot of work. Other mistakes are easy to make, which makes them extremely dangerous pitfalls that you will want to avoid at all costs.

People make mistakes because they do not know better. Once you read this book, you will no longer be able to claim ignorance. Read on and maybe you will not make the common mistakes that everyone else seems to make *over and over again.*

By learning from the mistakes of others, you will have a chance to minimize the small business failure rate. And you will have less heartache, since you will waste much less of your capital, your personal energy and your self-esteem.

CHAPTER ONE

CHAPTER TWO

MARKETING MISTAKES

WHAT IS MARKET-ING?

Marketing management involves all the activities in the business that are associated with:

► Deciding which products or services to offer to prospective customers.

► Offering prospects the opportunity to buy products and services, with the desired outcome being a sale.

It is the lifeblood of a business. Without effective marketing management, most businesses fail. In fact, the most frequently cited reason for the failure of businesses is the lack of effective marketing.

Marketing also includes everything from understanding the customers' needs, to determining how to fill those needs so that customers feel they have received a fair value for their dollars. This is the essence of a customer-driven business— everyone's thinking is guided by what the customer wants and needs. And successful businesses have a track record of satisfying their customers. This is what keeps the customers returning year after year. Satisfied customers are the best advertisement a business can have—the foundation of powerful word-of-mouth referrals that established business rely upon.

Word-of-mouth marketing only occurs after satisfied customers begin to spread the word. During start-up, businesses need other forms of promotion; once you have built a solid, customer-driven track record, referrals come more naturally.

Marketing also involves knowing what business your are in and setting goals for that business. If you do not know where you want to go, any road will do. If you want to be successful, you have to set goals and then spend the time, energy and capital necessary to get there.

PROMOTION

You must become knowledgeable about and comfortable with whatever promotional techniques you use to reach your goals. For example, if you choose to use direct mail to promote your business, learn all there is to know about direct mail; you do not want to misuse it and produce little or no results.

Regardless of the specific promotional technique you use, you want it to result in sales. Unless you sell, the promotional approach has not been successful. Somewhere in your marketing efforts, you must make the prospective customer interested in your products or services.

A *moment of truth* is when the customer has to make a decision whether or not he or she is interested enough to buy your product or service. This is when a potential sales can occur. This is also when customer service becomes critical. Customer service is the effort to keep customers happy, which is no small task. It is also one of the most important activities in your business, involving every employee—from the person who sends out bills, to the person who answers the phone, to the service department.

Everyone in your organization has a moment of truth with customers and prospective customers and it is collectively, all those moments of truth, that keep customers coming back or drive them away. Ultimately, someone in your small business will direct a customer's interest so he or she purchases your product. This is called a sale.

CASE STUDY

It's All In the Name

Choosing a name for an organization presents an opportunity to make an immediate impact. The business name is usually the first thing—similar to a newspaper headline— that a prospective customer notices. Consumers are bombarded by competitors. Getting them to stop and notice your company's name is important if you want them to inquire for your goods or services, or simply to remember who you are.

The Computer Solutions's case study reveals the importance of a business' name. Often, the business name is not given the scrutiny that is necessary to ensure it will work to grow the business. Use the business name to tell your story as briefly and powerfully as you can.

Three computer systems analysts, Dave, Ann and Jerry, formed a company that they decided to call Computer Solutions. Having entered the field in the early 1970s, the three partners all had mainframe computer systems backgrounds. Over the years, they had gained skills in personal computers and had become proficient in word processing, spreadsheets and database software.

They were inspired to go into business when they observed that over the years, as personal computer software became increasingly sophisticated, users in both large and small organizations frequently did not take advantage of the enhanced capabilities to address their various problems.

Computer Solutions was launched when the three partners decided to make a break from their full-time positions as computer analysts in large firms. They agreed that each would specialize in one area of expertise, which would allow them to cover a wide range of personal computer user problems and capabilities, using the available software.

They decided to market their firm to trade and professional associations and organizations that utilized personal computers as a principal means of doing business. These businesses were rapidly increasing in numbers as the business world moved toward buying more personal computers. They promoted Computer Solutions with a newsletter that described their services and offered solutions to typical software application problems.

At the time they started Computer Solutions, the computer systems analyst market in personal computers had become crowded. Start-up was difficult. Inquiries did not come pouring in and the partners wondered why, since they thought they were well positioned. They did a small business, but not at the level they had projected. After six months, all the partners were forced to take part-time work in as mainframe systems analysts. They continued to wonder why they were not getting more responses from the regular mailings of their promotional newsletter.

At one of their staff meetings, the discussion turned to the newsletter, the services they were offering and finally to the responses they were getting. After Jerry, who was fielding the calls, described typical calls, it became evident that many of their calls were for hardware solutions. Dave pressed Jerry for the number of the calls. To his great surprise, Jerry realized that most callers either wanted help with repairing of their computers or with adding of peripherals—software solutions.

The callers were mistaking Computer Solutions for a computer hardware firm, rather than a software outfit. Jerry had taken the calls, clarified what the firm did, and not thought further about the callers' confusion. The calls for hardware service far outnumbered those for software systems services; Jerry had never before noticed.

During the next week, all three partners fielded calls to determine why customers were calling them for hardware rather than software solutions. They found that callers thought of hardware first when they heard the name Computer Solutions, since the word *computer,* a hardware term, was predominant. In reality, the partners did nothing in the way of hardware sales or service.

Analysis

Why had the firm name hurt Computer Solutions's sales?

Just how important is an organization's name?

How much can a name help a firm grow?

The partners had chosen a name that they believed would help their business. It sounded good to them. From their story, it is apparent that the name did not serve them well. In fact, it completely misled prospective customers about the services the business provided. The partners thought that the name Computer Solutions would lead to prospective inquiries. It did, but they were not inquiries that would turn into business prospects and sales.

It was almost a year before they realized the impact of their name and how much it had hurt their promotional efforts. Because of the misleading name they had chosen— a name that did not describe the services or products that they supplied—they had missed out on nearly a year's worth of prospects.

The name Computer Solutions was a bad choice that had set back their efforts.

Lessons to be Learned

Names can and often do make the difference when it comes to gaining inquiries and sales. Choose your organization's name carefully. It is immeasurably important to the success of your business.

If your company has a bad name, is it worth going to the trouble to change it? You bet!

The name game is powerful when it comes to promoting your organization. If a name is not working for you, change it. Changing the name is also an opportunity to let current clients/customers know about your new services or products and to clarify your business purpose to prospects.

Naming your business can become a complex process. Registering a business's name that is protected by law can be expensive and can require assistance from a professional to determine if you can use a particular name. The effort involved in properly registering a name will be well worth your time.

Answer the following questions:

▶ List the three most important things that you want your prospects and customers to think of when they think of your company.

1.

2.

3.

▶ Does your company name tell your customers and prospects about the three things that you want your customers to think of when they think of your company?

▶ Do you think your business would improve if you changed the name?

See also *Marketing Your Consulting or Professional Services,* by David Karlson, Ph.D., Crisp Publications; *Improving Your Company Image,* by Sylvia Blishak, Crisp Publications.

CASE STUDY

A Mass Market Product Without a Mass Market Distribution Network

Many good businesses ideas are just that—good ideas. Converting a good idea into a successful business takes homework at every stage of the development of the business. Any step that is skipped jeopardizes the business's success and can almost assure failure.

Getting the product or service to market is a fundamental requirement for any business. In this case study, Mal and Frank have an idea about a business, but have trouble getting that idea to the right audience.

Mal was a noted authority on job hunting in his region of the country. As a former corporate trainer for several Fortune 500 companies, he knew his way around the corporate arena. And, his background in corporate training and personnel gave him an insider's view of what it takes to get hired.

Frank, one of Mal's job-hunting clients, was very impressed by Mal's approach to placement. With a background in media and advertising, Frank felt that there was a market for a job-hunting video. Frank was particularly impressed with Mal, and wanted to involve him in the project because Mal's system of job hunting had successfully landed Frank a job as the vice-president of a large corporation. He suggested to Mal that they coproduce a video on job hunting.

He agreed with Frank that a video on job hunting was sorely needed by job hunters, since so many white collar professionals were being laid off due to downsizing and the severe recession. Mal saw the potential for his career to take off on a national basis.

Mal and Frank formed a partnership with the idea that together they would underwrite the cost of producing the video. They both refinanced their homes to raise the $50,000 they needed to produce, package and assemble their inventory. They fleshed out the script and shopped for a studio that specialized in low-cost, high-quality videos. The production of the video took longer than they thought, but they wanted to take the time so it would be right. Their finished product cost more than they had anticipated. Attractively packaging was also more expensive than they had budgeted.

Once they had an inventory of videos, they began their sales efforts, targeting the masses of white collar workers who were looking for jobs. They had little capital left to market the video after they exceeded their production and packaging budgets.

They set the unit price of the video at $80, which they based on production costs and the initial inventory of the 1,000 videos they had contracted to buy. Unsuccessfully, they tried to market the video through two networks:

► Job-placement counselors

► Other interested parties that Frank drummed up in each major city

And they made personal appearances on talk shows in each major market and visited each of the networks that Frank set up in each major city.

Although everyone loved the video, sales were only on a one and two basis—well below the volume needed to justify the expense of production. Meanwhile, they were rapidly running out of funding. Travel expenses were eating up their precious savings, and they had achieved little results in the way of sales.

Finally, with only a couple hundred of the video sold, Mal and Frank were forced to sell the remaining inventory, at a fraction of the production costs, to investors who planned to mass market the video.

Analysis

Where did Mal and Frank go wrong?

Why didn't they sell more videos?

What should they have done to succeed?

Mal and Frank allowed themselves to be blinded by their great idea for a product:

► They did not have a mass market distribution channel, which is necessary to sell a product in volume. They had not explored methods to sell the thousands of videos necessary to fund their operation. Without the critical distribution channel, they lost everything.

► Mal's and Frank's idea seemed well founded. However, they did not do enough homework to check out their market. They based the retail price of the video on their costs, not on market demand. They did not find out what people would pay for a video on job hunting, and assumed that customers would value the video. They simply assumed that the video would be in demand, and overlooked the importance of how much unemployed professionals would consider to be the fair market value of a video. Considering that the best selling books on job hunting sell for only $10, their price tag might have been too high.

Lessons to Be Learned

Mal and Frank knew a lot about the product end of the business. What they *did not* know about was what killed them. Neither had the retail background necessary to sell the product, and this oversight is what eventually led to their downfall.

Their product was fairly innovative. Few videos on job hunting were on the market at the time they produced theirs. No doubt the market was wide open, but would consumers buy videos to help them search for a job?

Using a video to teach job-hunting skills would mean a change in behavior for the public. If your product or service represents a new way of doing things, prospects will have to behave differently. Getting prospective buyers to do something a new way is never easy, especially when it costs them more money than their old, familiar way.

Getting a product into the hands of the masses is no easy task, and Mal and Frank were not equipped for the job. Without an appropriate distribution system, they had no way to achieve the volume necessary to succeed. Mal and Frank's experience illustrates how important it is, when you are selling to a mass market, to find a distribution system *before one penny is spent on creating the inventory.*

Your Turn

Answer the following questions:

► Do you have a great idea for a product or service?

► Have you identified a target market?

► Do you have a distribution plan for your product?

See also *Writing and Implementing a Marketing Plan,* by Richard F. Gerson, Ph.D., Crisp Publications.

CASE STUDY

Consistently Inconsistent

Besides being committed to their product, business owners must be consistent in their promotion of the product. Promotion is one of the key ingredients of sales success. And consistent promotion requires investing in an ad campaign that conveys a certain offer or message until you think people have gotten the message and had sufficient time to respond.

If you fail to invest in promotion, you risk not growing the business. In this case study, we learn the value of ongoing, consistent promotion.

For several years, Rob had been the service manager for a large copier machine operation. He had an exceptional capacity to understand electronics. Every year he had come out number one in his class of the national, name-brand manufacturer's service school where new products servicing procedures were reviewed.

Over the years, Rob had tried to figure out how he might start his own business. He decided to open a television and VCR repair shop. To prepare, while he was still employed, Rob enrolled in self-instructional training courses.

After a couple of years of training, Rob met the owner of a small television repair shop who wanted to sell the business and retire. At the time, Rob did not have the money to buy the owner out. For the next couple of years, while the owner continued to try to sell his business, Rob spent his spare time working at the repair shop, learning the business. While he worked at the shop, he realized that if he were to someday buy the business and make a living there, it would need to grow.

Finally, Rob struck up a deal with the owner. Essentially, the two men reversed roles; Rob became the owner and the former-owner became the part-time employee. Their financial agreement appeared to meet both their needs. Within a year, Rob was able to quit his full-time job with the copier retailer and to dedicate his time to the repair shop.

The business seemed to go well, except that Rob never had enough business to pay all the bills. He decided to use promotion to grow the business. His goal was to bring prospects into the shop where they would see the repair operation, get to know Rob and build trust relationships.

Rob placed an insert that offered free cleaning for VCRs in the large metropolitan newspaper. Since he had several copier machines from his old job, Rob ran off the 10,000 copies of the insert himself. These were inserted into the metropolitan paper in the zip codes around the shop. The insert cost Rob $2,000, plus production costs.

The results were far below Rob's expectations; only twenty people brought in their VCRs for a free cleaning. He swore never to advertise again.

Analysis

Was Rob justifiably disappointed over the results of the insert advertisement?

What can you expect from an advertisement?

Is a one-shot promotional program effective?

Rob expected more than he got. He was looking for a quick fix, not committed to the long-term. When he did not get the results he expected, he blamed advertising, calling it a "rip off."

Rob's expectations were unrealistic, especially since he was not committed to using advertising on a regular basis. He had just started to get the word out about his high-quality, honest repair shop, and expected far too much from a single ad program. Twenty responses might even be considered very good for a starter ad. Rob canceled out, without giving his campaign a chance.

Advertising is not a quick-fix method to grow a business. It must be committed to on a long-term basis. To see what works, a business must take time to establish a track record with advertising. It needs to be repeated several times—this is known as an *ad campaign.*

Lessons to Be Learned

Promotional expenditures are a capital investment for which the business should get a return. Many new business owners expect too much from their initial promotional investments. Quickly discouraged, they pull back and refuse to promote further.

A business owner must be consistent and committed to the value of promotion. With a good promotional strategy, the more the business is promoted, the faster the business should grow. Consider promotion as a long-term investment—advertise consistently for a certain period of time to get the results you want. Then, if you have promoted well and results do not come, consider whether there is a demand for the product or service you are promoting.

Most successful companies have an advertising budget. They are keenly aware that if customers are going to buy their products and services, they must get their message across.

Your Turn

Answer the following questions:

► Detail four components in your promotional plan.

1. Promotion Budget: $ _____

2. Frequency of promotions: _____

3. Type Promotion: _____

4. Desired Results: _____

► Is your promotional program short-term or a long-term?

See also *Marketing Strategies for Small Businesses,* by Richard F. Gerson, Ph.D., Crisp Publications.

CASE STUDY

Bad Location, Bad Location

Many first-time business owners either underestimate the value of good retail space or are ignorant about the importance of their business' location. Determining a good location is critical to the success of the business. It requires careful attention and analysis.

This case study shows the importance of preparing and planning for the future when you establish your business. Ray's circumstances are extreme; most decisions are not so clear cut or obvious.

For eight years, Ray owned a business that sold audio components with a specialty in speakers from the same location. In addition to manufacturing speakers, he rebuilt them and sold all the parts necessary for customers to rebuild their own speakers.

When he started his company, he chose a warehouse location for both the retail store and the manufacturing of his own line of speakers. He thought of it as a great deal, since it gave him lots of space for warehousing and manufacturing.

The business grew slowly, but steadily. However, Ray was disappointed at the gross sales volume. When he wrote his original business plan, his research revealed a much greater potential volume of sales than he had achieved in his early years. To cover the work, he had to employ his wife and a part-time assistant who helped with both speaker manufacturing and retail sales.

Then, during the economic recession of the early 1990s, Ray's sales dropped dramatically. Ray could no longer afford to continue the promotion necessary to get people to come to his out-of-the-way factory and retail facility. Declining sales threatened Ray's ability to stay in business. Since there was no drive-by traffic, what had once appeared like a good price for rental space now threatened the existence of his business.

Ray barely held on. Once the worst of the recession passed, sales picked up again. Ray had nearly lost his business while he learned a critical lesson: *you get what you pay for in retail space.*

Analysis

Where did Ray go wrong?

What initial business location decisions got Ray into trouble?

What could Ray have done to make his business profitable?

How important is location to the success of a business?

Ray erred by being cheap when it came to retail space. He focused on manufacturing. He did not pay attention or know enough about the negative impact his location would have on selling the speakers that he manufactured.

When he started his business, Ray had not wanted to pay what appeared to be a premium for a good retail location. He only considered the square footage costs and ignored the additional costs he would have, to get people to visit his out-of-the-way location.

In the end, Ray actually spent more and had less to show for it. He had to pay for his promotions on a regular basis, which meant he spent more to get people into his showroom during recessionary times. Paradoxically, during recessionary times he had less—not more—to spend on promotion.

Having signed a five-year lease, Ray was stuck in a poor retail space that did benefit from drive-by traffic. Fortunately, he made it through this period of his lease. Then, having learned the hard way the importance of retail space, he moved to a new location on a busy highway with exceptional drive-by traffic.

His retails sales skyrocketed, due to his location and good signs. His unique idea for consumers to rebuild their own speakers was a huge success. He had a strong market in people with old speakers in beautiful cabinets who wanted to upgrade their speakers at a fraction of the cost of replacing them with speakers of similar capabilities.

Lessons to Be Learned

Large fast-food chains hire experts to analyze and select their retail locations. They use computer modeling and databases that can predict the best locations for particular types of businesses. Planning a business location has become a science. Since most start-up businesses cannot afford to hire experts, they analyze and plan their locations themselves. This can be dangerous, as Ray's experience shows. For retailers, it can be the most important business decision they make.

Regardless of the sophistication of the selection process, the approach to find retail space must take into account traffic patterns, parking, visibility from the highway, the socio-economic make up of the community, the businesses adjoining or nearby, and public transportation.

Answer the following questions:

▶ List five criteria that are important to the location of your business.

1.

2.

3.

4.

5.

▶ Where can you get help in selecting appropriate retail space for your business?

See also *Your New Business: A Personal Plan For Success,* by Charles L. Martin, Ph.D., Crisp Publications.

CASE STUDY

Can You Hold, Please?

The way in which the phones are answered is often the first and only impression a prospect or customer has of your company. Whether the experience is positive or negative, the effect can create business or diminish it.

This case study illustrates just how detrimental poor telephone manners can be to a business.

For years, Bill worked in the office-furniture industry, beginning right after college when he worked in the marketing department at the corporate headquarters of a large furniture manufacturer. While there, he learned the furniture business "from A to Z"—from manufacturing to sales and service in the field, at corporate-owned retail outlets.

Bill also worked with the furniture manufacturer's large dealer network, visiting with dealers and learning the secrets to owning a dealership. That's when he first thought about owning his own dealership.

Fifteen years later, Bill had the opportunity to buy a small furniture dealership in a growth area of the country. He put together a good business proposal and convinced the bank loan officer to give him the capital he required. The bank based the positive response on Bill's knowledge of office equipment retailing, plus the current owner's willingness to assist him.

Bill inherited a pretty good staff from the former owner. He kept most of them on as employees, since they knew the customers very well and had been part of the former business' success story.

However, when the receptionist left, Bill had to hire a someone to take over the position. He rewrote the job description to include a considerable amount of functions in addition to answering the phone, incorporating some accounting duties into the responsibilities. Carol was selected from the many candidates who applied for the position.

At about the same time, Bill started an aggressive marketing campaign to generate more telephone inquires for office equipment sales. As a result, the phones rang more frequently than ever.

Carol was very busy with her accounting duties, and she got along well with everyone in accounting. She tried to answer the phone by the third ring, but usually had to put callers on hold. As Bill increased his promotion to beef up sales, Carol received more calls inquiring about office furniture. And the more calls that came in, the longer the callers had to wait.

Over a period of months, Bill started to hear feedback during sales calls that he and his sales staff made on the prospects who had inquired by phone. Fairly consistently, they described their first experience with his company as negative: they had waited on hold for up to five minutes. From their first encounter, they began to form a negative impression of the company because of the way their telephone calls had been handled.

Bill was surprised at the feedback he heard. He had not realized that calls were not being answered in a timely fashion. That started him wondering about how many other callers might have hung up, impatient with being put on hold for so long.

When questioned, Carol admitted that the little red blinking HOLD light on her telephone console went out more often than she could get back to the callers. Two members of the sales staff told him that they met with great resistance to lining up follow-up sales calls, after they took calls from callers who had been put on hold for too long. Frequently, they found the attitude of the callers hostile from the beginning of their phone conversations.

Bill vowed to change this. He realized he had to do something about the typical answer Carol gave to callers on busy days: "Thank you for calling. Can I put you on hold?"

Analysis

How badly was Bill's company hurt by the way they implemented their telecommunications program?

How important is that moment of truth when a prospective customer calls on your company—especially in response to a promotional effort?

What can Bill do now provide better telephone customer service?

It is difficult to calculate just how much damage was done to Bill's company by the way the telephone was handled. To estimate, you can multiply the average number of calls

(32) received in Bill's sales department daily, times 22, the number working days each month. The total is a whopping 704 calls. Multiplying this by twelve, we can estimate a grand total of 8,448 calls a year.

Each of these 8,448 calls is a moment of truth, an opportunity for Bill's business to make a first impression to a prospective customer. You can see from this simple calculation that the damage by telephone can be significant.

It is absolutely critical to monitor the receptionist function—which is often the first impression you are making—at all times. You need to show callers that their calls are important. Do not put them on hold for more than thirty seconds or they will likely come away thinking of their experiences as negative. And negative first impressions are hardly the way to begin positive relationships that could result in sales.

What can Bill do to improve the callers' first impressions? He needs to reassess Carol's duties and make answering of telephone calls of top priority. He may need to add more phone lines and more sales and service staff to respond to inquiries in a more timely way.

Being geared up for business means being able to do business with your prospective customers when they want to communicate with you. This is good customer service; in this case, it needs to happen on the telephone.

Lessons to Be Learned

The importance of quality customer service, especially on the telephone, cannot be overstated. If you do not provide good customer service, your prospects will find one of your competitors who does.

A misused telephone can have devastating results, while a properly handled telephone offers a tremendous potential for success. How the phone is answered, how long it takes to connect the caller with the appropriate staff member, and how that staff member handles the telephone call are each moments of truth. And how those moments of truth come out add up to how successful your business is at gaining new customers.

Your Turn

Answer the following questions:

- ► How many calls does your business receive each month?
- ► How many callers hang up each day when they have to wait too long to speak with the appropriate person?
- ► Have you set standards for answering the telephone in your company? Do your employees understand the standards, and follow them?

See also *Telephone Courtesy and Customer Service,* by Lloyd C. Finch, Crisp Publications; *Telemarketing Basics,* by Julie Freestone, Crisp Publications; *The Telephone and Time Management,* by Dru Scott, Ph.D., Crisp Publications.

CASE STUDY

My Business Is All Seasonal

Knowing all of the details of the business you are entering is crucial to the success of your business. Jack's experience in the next case study illustrates how important this is.

Jack and Karen have a large and growing family. Four years ago he injured his back on the job. He immediately had to make a lot of changes in his life. Karen, who was not working outside the home at the time, found a job so they could make ends meet. Jack started a travel agency in their home, where he was available to take care of the children.

Through his participation in the church and through parents he met through his children's school, Jack was well connected in the community. He was also a good salesman. Two months after starting the travel agency, he had a solid client base and his prospects looked great. He invested in some basic office equipment, installed a telephone line for the business, and spent a lot of time on the telephone looking for more clients.

In September, his income suddenly dropped to nothing. School started and the vacation business, which had been his income source, dried up. By October, he was having trouble paying his bills. His financial troubles escalated in November, when he had to dig into savings to make the mortgage payment on the house.

Analysis

What happened to Jack's business?

Why did sales dry up?

What could Jack have done to avoid such a severe slump in sales?

Jack had the right idea for a start-up business, but did not anticipate the seasonal nature of the market. If the terrific summer market would have carried him through the winter—or until he was able to establish a winter market—he could have survived much better.

But Jack never established a winter travel market, and he did not have a big enough summer season to carry him over into the next summer season. He had not anticipated the nature of his market.

Jack did not understand the nuances of the travel agency business. That cost him dearly. Had he researched the nature of the travel agent industry, he would have realized that it is seasonal, particularly with family travel. Had he realized this, he could have attempted to develop some commercial accounts early on, which would have given him revenue during the seasons when the family travel business dried up. He would have avoided the seasonal nature of family travel and his business would have survived.

Lessons to Be Learned

When entering into a businesses market, make sure you understand how that market works:

- ► Is it seasonal?
- ► Is it price driven?
- ► Is it service driven?

The behavior that is unique to the market you are considering is critical to your business's survival. If you do not understand the market you are attempting to enter, you will put yourself at risk just like Jack.

Jack's mistake was when he overlooked the very nature of the travel industry market. When investigating a potential business and market, be sure you explore and uncover the basics of that business and market. Inquire about the consumers of the products or services, how they use the products or services, and as much as you can about how things work.

Your Turn

Answer the following questions:

- ► Have you thoroughly researched the market that you plan to enter?
- ► Do you know the unique nature of your market?

See also *Marketing Strategies for Small Businesses,* by Richard F. Gerson, Ph.D., Crisp Publications; *Marketing Your Consulting or Professional Services,* by David Karlson, Ph.D., Crisp Publications.

CASE STUDY

No Response—No Confidence

When using direct-mail promotions, a single variable can completely ruin the outcome. You need to take into account everything from the layout and design to the copy, the timeliness of the piece, and the cost involved.

In this case study, Professor Anvar's mistake illustrates how the timing of direct-mail advertising can undermine the success of the promotion, as well as the success of the business.

With a doctoral degree in computer science, Professor Anvar was a tenured member of the teaching staff in the computer science program of a major university. Over the years, while still in his comfortable and secure higher-education nest, he was able to get an insider's view of the business world. Professor Anvar saw great possibilities for himself in the private sector. When opportunity knocked, he responded.

He launched a company that specialized in unique personal computer software applications. In no time, his firm grew. It was publicly traded and became known as one of the fast-track high technology firms for investors to watch.

Meanwhile, the professor had not lost his love of teaching. He launched a series of seminars aimed at his type of users—mostly federal department employees, with whom he had been very successful in creating software applications.

He launched the series with a direct-mail campaign that consisted of a skillfully designed brochure that announced the seminars. Professor Anvar expected to hear from 1 percent of the 25,000 potential participants who were sent the brochure packet. That would have brought him 250 seminar participants—a reasonable expectation.

In fact, the professor was dumbfounded when he did not receive one response from the brochures, which he had spent $10,000 producing and mailing. After much deliberation, Professor Anvar decided to forget about doing seminars. Yet, he continued to wonder why absolutely no one had registered for even one of the eight seminars he had offered.

Analysis

Numerous variables can effect the response rate of a direct mail campaign. Professor Anvar's response rate is almost unheard of; by chance alone someone usually responds.

Then, what went wrong? After much analysis and careful consideration, one variable surfaced as the cause of Professor Anvar's zero seminar response rate. The timing of his seminars was completely out of sync with the federal budget cycle. He scheduled the seminars for the last month of the federal budget year. Potential participants had no funding left for training. He had not anticipated that the federal sector plans training far in advance—sometimes as much as a year in advance. So no one had funding available at the time that the professor scheduled his seminars.

Lessons to Be Learned

Unfortunately, when the professor planned his seminar series, he did not think about timeliness. The mistake cost him $10,000.

Promotional tactics used to promote businesses are much more complex in nature than they seem on the surface. In this case, the direct-mail promotion may or may not have been right on target; the variable that was not accounted for was the one that went wrong. Had the timing been right, since this was a new, untested seminar program, it would still have been possible for the results to have been disappointing.

Far too often, small business owners dive right in, thinking that they can use promotional techniques successfully the first time. The professor's case study is an example of how risky these techniques can be, if they are not carefully planned.

If you do not have experience with the promotional effort you are using, treat it as an experiment. Until you have established a successful record, consider the results of your promotional efforts to be hit and miss. You must be in the game for the long run—not for a one-shot deal.

Your Turn | ***Answer the following questions:***

► List the promotional techniques you have experience with:

1.

2.

3.

4.

5.

► List the promotional techniques you don't have experience with, and would like to try:

1.

2.

3.

4.

5.

See also *Direct Mail Magic,* by Charles Mallory, Crisp Publications; *Marketing Your Consulting or Professional Services,* by David Karlson, Ph.D., Crisp Publications.

CASE STUDY

Answer the Door When Opportunity Knocks

To succeed, an entrepreneur must be focused. And he or she cannot be focused on more than one business. Opportunist behavior, which is fine in an established company, is lethal in a start-up business. It greatly intensifies the risks inherent in a new business, because it provides a constant source of distraction from the job of launching a successful business—one successful business. If you focus all of your energy on just one business, your business has a chance of succeeding.

In this cases study, Ed, a new entrepreneur, tries to do too much too fast. Ed's energies are spread thinly across all of his interests and activities.

A graduate of Harvard in public policy, Ed worked for years as a policy analyst at the Environmental Protection Agency in Washington, DC. More recently, he went to work for a large private consulting firm. The firm bid on all types of government contracts. Since his proposals were successful in getting contracts, Ed was considered to be one of their best proposal writers. He could visualize opportunities for the firm in just about every request for proposal (RFP) that was publicized within the areas of the firm's collective expertise and experience.

Like so many professionals who work in consulting firms, Ed recognized that the principals of the firm make the big money, while the staff—although well compensated—burns out in the chase for the big government bucks.

As he gained experience, especially in writing successful proposals, Ed saw no reason that he could not start his own consulting firm. At the age of 45, fairly typical for starting a consulting business, Ed launched his own firm. He had saved enough money for start-up, which meant he would be able to cover his bills until he expected that he could generate income.

Ed saw nothing but opportunities for his firm, and he pursued them all. He launched a business-mediation practice with a partner. He responded to government RFPs in the environment area. He acquired all the equipment necessary to launch a highly specialized computer mapping service. He also taught two graduate courses each semester in a master's program.

What is important to realize is that each of Ed's pursuits was distinctly different from the previous and the next: essentially, Ed launched three different businesses.

As the months passed by, many of the opportunities that Ed thought were there did not materialize. When they did, the contracts were small and hardly worth the effort; they took so much of Ed's time to complete, he had little or no time left to pursue the growth of each of his businesses.

After a year, Ed had to admit that opportunity-seeking was not working for him. The level of income that he had hoped to generate was not there. He found it increasingly difficult to pay his bills. And all the specialized equipment for computer mapping sat unused.

With little success, Ed tried harder to network for the three businesses. The national economic downturn had affected even the normally stable Washington, DC, market and the situation grew increasingly hopeless for Ed. His efforts to generate business did not even generate enough income to pay his bills.

Analysis

Where did Ed go wrong?

Why did his opportunistic style, which had worked so well in the large consulting firm, not work with his own business?

Ed thought he could launch three business at once. This is a classic mistake for new business owners. In fact, it is just about all you can do to launch one business successfully. He stacked the odds against himself by trying to do too many things. As a result, he did not have the time or energy to dedicate to any one of the businesses.

Ed failed to recognize the shift in his behavior that he would have to make to succeed in his own business. In fact, when things got really bad, he stepped up his efforts to do what he thought would help; unfortunately, he only intensified his troubles when he intensified his pursuit of even more divergent opportunities.

It takes a monumental effort to start up a business. All the stories you might have heard about the long hours and endless effort it takes are true. To get a business to catch on and be successful is no small achievement. And trying to start more than one at a time is just too much to handle. People who stay focused will have the greatest chance of success. Opportunistic behavior patterns must be laid aside until the start-up business has caught on.

Lessons to Be Learned

Know yourself and know what it takes to succeed as a start-up business. This is one of the most difficult undertakings you can imagine. The main reason so many new businesses fail is that the owners do not commonly have experience starting a new business.

New business owners need to avoid opportunistic behavior like a plague. It could hurt any chance they have to succeed. The idea of creating a lot of possibilities is tempting, but it is almost always fatal. Ask Ed.

The margin for success in a new business is very narrow and does not allow for costly mistakes. Those who succeed become members of a very special club.

Your Turn	**Answer the following questions:**

► List any opportunist behaviors that you have that could get in the way of your ability to stay focused.

1.

2.

3.

4.

► Can you stay focused on one task or project for long periods of time?

See also *Finding Your Purpose: A Guide to Personal Fulfillment,* by Barbara J. Braham, Crisp Publications; *Organizational Vision, Values and Mission,* by Cynthia Scott, Ph.D., Dennis T. Jaffe, Ph.D., and Glenn Tobe, Crisp Publications.

ASK YOURSELF

▶ How well (or poorly) does your company name and location work for you?

▶ Describe your market's needs and the steps you have taken (or plan to take) to ensure that your product is understood and valued by your prospects.

▶ What questions do you need to have answered about your market that will give you the information necessary to minimize risk?

▶ Clarify the steps you have taken (or will take) to promote your business and get your product into the hands of consumers?

▶ Portray your plans and expectations for any promotions you plan.

CHAPTER
THREE

PERSONNEL
MISTAKES

WHAT EFFECTS ARE YOUR EMPLOY-EES HAVING?

Each person in a small business is crucial to the success of the company. Unlike large businesses, where the behavior of any one employee does not have serious consequences, most small businesses cannot withstand even one bad employee. Similar to a family, a small business is a very small working unit. When the unit is functional, major results can be achieved; when the unit is dysfunctional, the results can be catastrophic and can cause the business to fail.

Since each person can make such a tremendous difference in reaching the goals of the small business, selection of partners, sales staff and clerks is critical to the small business. Once they are hired, the ways that employees are treated, managed and paid play an important role in ensuring that the employees make a positive contribution.

The case studies in this chapter are examples of the variety of hiring, managing and compensating mistakes that business owners can make in the highly complex world of employing people.

CASE STUDY

Good Intentions, Bad Results

Regardless of how enthusiastic an employee of a small firm is, he or she needs to be given both responsibility and authority to be productive. In this case study, Arlene learns that she cannot expect her employee to do his job if she has not given him the authority. Luckily for her, she learned before it was too late.

Arlene owns a small temporary personnel agency that supplies clerical help to local businesses. Her experience as director of personnel for a middle-sized company had given her a strong background on the various clerical positions that businesses may require.

When she first struck out on her own, Arlene hired Ann as her clerical/secretarial assistant. Ann served as her right hand and could almost read Arlene's mind when decisions needed to be made. As the company grew, Arlene realized that she had to hire someone who could support her and serve as second in command to deal with her clients. She needed a professional whom she could groom to run the business whenever she was away.

Ann ran advertisements, collected resumes and conducted interviews. From the candidates, she decided to hire Tim, a hard-charger who came on board full of enthusiasm. Tim seemed like a real shot-in-the-arm for the business. Hoping that he would learn the entire business operation, Arlene gave him a lot of responsibility, which he accepted gladly.

All went well at first. Tim was creative, and he looked for new and better ways to tackle all his assignments. Arlene traveled more, and she was able to serve more remote clients by leaving Tim in charge of the office. However, when she returned she began to notice that the office was not being run the same way as she had run it.

As the months passed, Arlene became increasingly upset with Tim. From her perspective, he seemed to be doing the job his own way, without regard to any of the procedures she had put into place. And Ann, her trusted assistant, would not take direct orders from Tim in Arlene's absence; instead, she made excuses for not following Tim's directives. Arlene finally confronted Tim about the approach he was taking to run the business. Tim was shocked—he had thought he was doing a great job.

After Arlene and Tim aired their differences, Tim began to question his ability to contribute to the company without being able to be creative. As time passed, friction in the office got worse and worse, with Tim seen as the bad guy. He eventually considered quitting.

When Arlene realized how bad the situation was, she suggested she and Tim meet again. A breakthrough that occurred during that discussion of the misunderstanding changed Arlene's thinking about how she managed people. Arlene suddenly understood that, although she had given Tim responsibility to get the job done, she had not given him the authority he needed to be in charge when she was gone. Without authority, Tim had become a puppet who was unable to do the job she had hired him to do.

Analysis

Where had Arlene failed as Tim's boss?

What are some keys to managing staff so that they are productive?

How important is it to give an employee authority and responsibility?

Arlene knew how to manage—she had managed large staffs in her old corporate job. Yet, she was so invested in her own business, and she wanted to control everything so badly, that she forgot the basics of managing staff effectively.

Fortunately for Arlene, she recognized what could have been a disastrous mistake. If she had not met with Tim to discuss their problem, she would have probably lost him. He would have moved on and she would have been left wondering what had happened.

Lessons to Be Learned

Each employee is very important to the success of a small business. There are no second- and third-string teams to jump in, so a small business has no room for personnel oversights.

That first team must be *empowered:* given the responsibility and the authority to do the job. And, within the guidelines that you set, each employee must be able to do the job in his or her way. Successful businesses recognize how important it is to fully empower employees.

Answer the following questions:

▶ Are you willing to give up your authority over the daily operations of your business?

▶ Is there someone to whom you can relinquish authority or must you be in charge all the time?

See also *Delegating for Results,* by Robert B. Maddux, Crisp Publications; *Empowerment: A Practical Guide for Success,* by Dennis T. Jaffe, Ph.D. and Cynthia Scott, Ph.D., Crisp Publications; *Rate Your Skills as a Manager: A Crisp Assessment Book,* Crisp Publications.

CASE STUDY

Overpaid Staff, Underpaid Owner

Many small business owners get themselves into trouble by giving bonuses and benefits that their faithful employees come to expect. Torn between loyalty and productivity, owners often resign themselves to paying dearly to keep good employees and keep them happy.

In this case study, Al had the misfortune of spending too much on salaries; without equating those salaries to profits, he lost his business.

Al had owned his sheet metal fabricating business for five years. His company specialized in making small metal parts that were part of a larger assembly. It had grown very nicely, and he had ten employees who were highly productive and loyal to the company. The hard-working employees had stayed with Al through good and bad times, and Al rewarded them very well.

To stay competitive Al also bought the latest steel fabricating machinery; these cost him dearly. He believed that he would not be able to bid jobs at competitive prices if he did not buy the fancy presses.

Eventually, the high wages he paid to the loyal staff and the constant expenses to update his equipment left Al little personal return on his investment. He became increasingly disillusioned, feeling like he was working for his employees and the equipment manufacturers, rather than the other way around.

Eventually, Al considered selling his business—the thing he loved most in the world. He became depressed and began to drink heavily. As the fiscal year-end approached, Al's accountant informed him that there was no profit for Al after all the business's bills had been paid. This was when Al decided to sell his business.

Analysis

Where did Al go wrong?

How could Al have make his business profitable?

Is it worth the trouble and risk to own a small business?

Al's heart was in the right place when he wanted to pay his employees very well, but his finances revealed that he was spending too much on salaries. He got himself into a predicament by paying for employee loyalty and faithfulness instead of relative productivity—profits and revenues.

As a result, Al did not have the money to pay himself what he merited. Ironically, considering his investment in the company and the reasonable return he should have been making, his employees had no idea that Al was making so little.

It took Al a number of years to get himself into this fix. If he had been willing to stay and to put a reasonable cap on employee incomes, it would have taken some time, but he might have been able to make a success of the business.

Lessons to Be Learned

Businesses need to achieve a balance between salaries—and benefits and bonuses—and profits. Al was not able to achieve this balance. He started to lose control of his business when he began to pay his employees too much. As a result, he lost his excitement for the business.

There is a fine line between salaries and profitability. Make sure you can tell the difference between what is enough and what is too much.

Your Turn

Answer the following questions:

► Is your employee compensation package fair and reasonable—for you and for your employees?

► If you are paying too much for loyalty and productivity, list four steps you will take to get the balance under control.

1.

2.

3.

4.

See also *Understanding Financial Statements,* by James O. Gill, Crisp Publications; *Budgeting for a Small Business,* by Terry Dickey, Crisp Publications; *The Basics of Budgeting,* by Terry Dickey, Crisp Publications.

CASE STUDY

Limited Staff—Limited Productivity

There is a time in the life span of most businesses when the owner must do the work of two people. This usually goes on until the owner feels comfortable hiring another full-time employee.

It takes a leap of faith to add another staff person. That person might even make more money than you! But once the new employee is on board, the owner has time to market the business, to increase the number of clients and to raise his or her income level. The owner also gains someone to delegate projects to that would otherwise not be completed in a timely fashion.

In this case study, Ellen faces the age-old problem: how to increase production capacity without adding significant employee expenses.

After graduating from a prestigious East Coast school of design, Ellen landed a job in a highly successful graphic design firm. She gained valuable experience there and, after five years, left to work for a large public relations firm.

Ellen found greater creative opportunities at the public relations firm. After two years, she was promoted to creative director. She thrived in the position, where her responsibilities included managing the entire graphic design staff. Ellen became well known for both her creative and her management abilities.

After five more years of hard work and sacrifice, Ellen decided to strike out on her own. With money she had saved, she launched a graphic design firm. Based upon her terrific reputation, she was able to get off to a fairly strong start by attracting some of her former clients.

Unfortunately, Ellen did not yet have any staff who she could delegate to, since she did not have enough revenue to justify hiring another graphic designer. She ended up on the drawing board much of the time and found herself in a "Catch 22": she could not make enough money to hire another designer, so she had to do all the design work herself; she did not have enough time to go out and bring in new business, because she was always having to fulfill the graphic design contracts she had already sold.

As a result, Ellen began to burn out and became disheartened about her business. It started to look like her great start was as far as she could go.

Analysis

What went wrong for Ellen?

Why couldn't Ellen continue to grow her small business?

What does it take to get ahead in a small business?

Like so many start-up companies, Ellen got off to a great start. She knew the right people and had the skills to deliver outstanding work. In fact, she was doing such a great job delivering outstanding graphic design projects to her clients that she did not have time to bring in new business.

Ellen could not produce quick-and-dirty work; she delivered only top-class graphic design to her clients. No matter how much clients pay, that level of work takes time.

Her dilemma was how to make more money while continuing to deliver top-quality work and how to bring in enough top-quality work to justify hiring more staff. Then she would be able to take the time to market her graphic design services to prospective clients.

Ellen's mistake was not knowing how to grow the business beyond herself. She needed to break the barrier of getting enough additional business to hire another graphic designer. And she could not get over this hurdle because she was burned out.

To expand their businesses, small business owners must have the confidence to risk answering "yes" to this important question: "Will I be able to get enough business to pay a new staff member each week before I pay myself?"

Lessons to Be Learned

If you do not grow your business, you are saddled with doing everything, all the time, every day. If that is okay with you, you do not need to think of Ellen's mistake as a mistake. However, if you want to be able to grow your business beyond yourself, you need to figure out exactly how you are going to do that.

Many small business owners use part-time help before they hire permanent staff. Many professionals are interested in doing part-time work. The challenge is to find part-time help who can live up to your standards. And finding good people quickly is no easy task.

Your Turn

Answer the following questions:

► Are you enjoying your business as much now as you were when you first started it?

► List five sources of quality staff for your business.

1.

2.

3.

4.

See also *Balancing Home and Career: Skills for Successful Life Management,* by Pamela J. Conrad, Crisp Publications; *Consulting For Success: A Practical Guide for Prospective Consultants,* by David Karlson, Ph.D., Crisp Publications.

CASE STUDY

The Isolation Syndrome—Working at Home Can Be Extremely Lonely

When you change your working environment dramatically, you can expect it will have an impact on your productivity. Some people thrive on being on their own; others find it takes a tremendous adjustment.

The isolation that comes from being on your own is especially acute in start-up situations, when the volume of business is often not enough to keep you busy. You really must know yourself; depending on your temperament, the adjustment to working alone can seem either short or quite long.

In this case study, Larry ran into some of the pitfalls of isolation until, eventually, he found some workable solutions.

For thirty years, Larry had worked as a trainer and as the head of training for a prestigious federal government agency. He was a good trainer and had looked forward to starting his own training firm when he retired.

When he did retire, Larry invested a considerable sum in computer equipment, office furniture, a fax machine, telephone equipment, etc. To Larry, spending money on equipment was a sign of his commitment to his new business.

Hoping that he would benefit from the networking opportunities, Larry became an active member of the professional society for training. Although he attended professional meetings, he soon found that most other members were equally hungry for business, and unwilling to share information that led to business.

As time passed, Larry was not getting a lot of training business, and he spent a lot of time at his home office, with no one to talk with. It was not long before he began to dread the mornings, the time when he had hoped to be happily at work. With no one to bounce ideas off of, he felt increasingly isolated.

Larry had been a terrific team player, and he was used to contributing to the betterment of the team, not to his personal advancement. Prior to his "retirement," he had spent his career working daily with dozens of people and serving on various committees. The networking opportunities in his own business were not like working at the office.

He made fewer sales calls each day and became increasingly isolated and less productive. He invented all kinds of creative excuses to avoid working in his home office. As a result, his training practice began to move backward instead of forward. He considered throwing in the towel as his discouragement grew.

Analysis

Larry had started out so enthusiastically about going into business for himself. What happened to change that?

What contributed to Larry's loss of productivity?

What could Larry have done to avoid the isolation he found working alone?

Larry was not used to working alone. As much as he networked, it was not the same as working with others. After thirty years of working as a team player, it was extremely hard for him to make the transition to working on his own.

Many new business owners never make that transition. They need the energy that is generated by working with others. If you are an extrovert, be wary of working on your own—you will have the greatest adjustment.

One way of dealing with the isolation of a new business is to form limited partnerships with others in the situation. Partnering can bring everyone great energy. Some small business owners find that they have more energy and can grow their businesses faster within successful partnerships.

You can choose partners whose skills complement those you do or do not have. For example, if you do not like to do marketing, you can find a partner who thrives on bringing in new business. Your responsibility will be to perform the work you are contracted for.

Can you partner? Are you willing to share the profits?

Larry could have used a partner. In fact, he later turned around his practice when he found a limited partner. She was also in training and liked getting business. Since Larry liked doing the training, they were able to come to an agreement that served them both well.

You may want to have several joint venture partners. You do not even have to form a legal partnership to do business together. However, it *is* best to put something in writing once you come to an agreement, to be sure you communicate to each other exactly what each of you expect—what the deal is.

Lessons to Be Learned

Each new business owner has to find out for him or herself what it is like to work alone. If it is too isolating for you, make sure you act quickly to find partnering opportunities. For those who do not have time to get used to being on their own, partnering offers an opportunity to avoid the pitfalls of low productivity and potential failure.

Your Turn

Answer the following questions:

► Are you more of a team player or an independent player?

► List five qualities you would look for in a partner.

1.

2.

3.

4.

5.

See also *Consulting For Success: A Practical Guide for Prospective Consultants,* by David Karlson, Ph.D., Crisp Publications; *Goals and Goal Setting,* by Larrie Rouillard, Crisp Publications.

CASE STUDY

Know Thyself—Real Well!

In business-to-business sales, you are often required to call on prospects and engage them before they will make a commitment to buy your products or services. This is one ability you either need to have, or you need to find an alternative solution, such as partnering, to substitute for your own expertise.

In this case study, Martin made the mistake of recognizing his personal shortcoming too late. This shortcoming became critical to the success of his business.

Martin had been a successful electrical engineer. He had also held positions in prestigious consulting firms that have offices all over the country. In each new situation, he learned the ropes quickly. He also realized that the major financial rewards go to the business owner.

Martin decided to leave his full-time position and to work part-time for a smaller consulting firm while he explored various possibilities for starting his own company. Since he was intrigued with telecommunications, he pursued voice-mail hardware companies, thinking he might become their local representative. At considerable cost to him, he trained on one company's equipment. Meanwhile, he explored a variety of other possibilities, looking at all types of telecommunications equipment. The more he looked, the more he found.

The specific idea for his own business developed slowly. Martin thought small businesses and professional service providers (lawyers, doctors, accountants) would be a perfect market for voice mail. The product would give them more flexibility in receiving and returning phone calls; their overheads would lower, since they would not need to hire as much help.

Martin became a distributor for a voice-mail system. However, after some effort, he found that there was limited demand for the product. Prospects did not want to spend as much as the system cost. Larger prospects were buying from larger distributors who had more complex equipment.

Sales did not materialize. Sadly, Martin folded his tent, gave up on his business idea and went back to work for a large consulting firm. The firm was happy to have this steady producer back in their stable.

Analysis

Where did Martin go wrong?

What kind of start-up mistakes did Martin make?

Martin was an engineer. He thought he could become a businessperson, but never acquired business savvy. Although he did product research, he did not do market research; before he jumped in, he did not find out what customers want and need and what they are willing to pay.

Martin could not bring himself to get out and shake hands with prospects and find out what they were thinking and what problems they faced. He was convinced he had a good idea, and did not test it until it was too late. Had he vigorously field-tested his idea, he would have established that there was not a market for the product he represented.

If the business had been viable, he could have also considered taking on a partner to deal with the sales end of the business. That would have meant he could concentrate on the technical end—his love. When you have an achilles heel like Martin did, you must shore it up. The most logical way is with a partner or, if you have enough capital, you can hire an employee to fill in the skills you do not have.

By the time Martin realized the make-up of his target market, he had already spent his capital on training and gathering his modest inventory. His only choice was to close his business.

Lessons to Be Learned

Martin did not know himself or what it takes to succeed in business. So, in a way he was destined to failure.

Sometimes, the only way to discover if you have it in you to succeed in business is to try. That was Martin's approach. If you assess your skills and see where you are strong and where you are weak, you minimize your costs and risks. If your weaknesses far outweigh the strengths required to succeed in business (e.g., marketing savvy, a head for business, etc.), you have a better idea about the odds for your success.

Can you afford not to know yourself and not to know what it takes to succeed as a small business owner?

Your Turn

Answer the following questions:

▶ List the skills required to succeed in your own business.

1.

2.

3.

4.

5.

6.

▶ List ten of your strengths and ten of your weaknesses that affect your ability to succeed in your own business.

	STRENGTHS	WEAKNESSES
1.		
2.		
3.		
4.		
5.		
6.		
7.		
8.		
9.		
10.		

See also *Consulting For Success: A Practical Guide for Prospective Consultants,* by David Karlson, Ph.D., Crisp Publications; *Finding Your Purpose: A Guide to Personal Fulfillment,* by Barbara J. Braham, Crisp Publications.

ASK YOURSELF

▶ Compare the appropriate number of employees for your business with your current number of employees. Include a discussion of how you have delegated the necessary authority to your employees.

▶ Describe the impact your employees' compensation package has on your profits.

▶ What personnel growth plans have you made for your business?

▶ How comfortable are your at letting someone else share the reins of your business?

CHAPTER FOUR

MANAGEMENT MISTAKES

THE ENTRE- PRENEUR ROLE

The management role of the president/principal/owner is probably the single most critical role in a small business. This individual sets the direction and goals for the business.

He or she is the entrepreneur, who comes up with the vision of where the business needs to go if it is to be financially successful. This is the same person who leads and directs all the employees in the small business. Therefore, he or she is also responsible for day-to-day operations—a role that is very different from being the company visionary.

Since the owner makes all the key decisions for the small business, he or she is responsible for its success or failure. Marketing and finance are two of several areas in which small business owners frequently lack sufficient experience, since they previously worked as specialists for other people before they started their own businesses. As a result, they generally do not have the experience needed to make well-informed decisions in the areas with which they are unfamiliar.

The demands of running and growing a small business will soon expose any achilles heel in a president/owner. It is best to find out your weaknesses early, so you can develop expertise or get help in these areas.

The case studies in this chapter reveal the results of various small business owners' weaknesses and mistakes in judgment.

CASE STUDY

The Missing Market

One of the greatest mistake a business owner can make is to assume there is a market for his or her idea. Frequently, the missing links are first not checking to see if there is a market, and then not exploring how to sell to that market. This is especially true when the product or service is innovative and people need to be educated about it before they are prepared to buy in or financially sponsor it.

In this case study, Ray's and Albert's partnership failed because neither of them took the time to research the market before they plunged in over their heads.

For fifteen years, Ray had been a highly successful high school social studies teacher. During eight of those years, he wrote a new type of social studies textbook, which was published by a major publisher and became a best seller in a tough market.

With his enhanced reputation as an author, Ray left teaching and became a consultant to school systems in social studies. His reputation grew from the increasing popularity of his textbook and his work as a consultant. He wrote other books and numerous articles. He used his reputation to bring him enough work to keep him quite busy.

After his books had been on the market for some time, Ray's popularity began to wane. He missed the special feeling he got from accomplishing something really big. He wanted to do something even bigger, especially after he experienced what being an author had done for his reputation and his pocketbook.

While he was networking, Ray met Albert. Albert had a varied career, and was especially skilled in video production. He had produced a lot of videos that made elected officials look especially good to their constituents.

Anxious for a change, Albert left the video studio he was working for on Capital Hill in Washington, DC. This was just before Albert and Ray became the best of friends, and had the idea to use video to create a new program for high school students to learn world news.

One night, after lots of beers and brainstorming, their idea took shape. They would create a news chronicle for high school students that presented the news the way kids would want to hear the news. Their backgrounds were perfect for the undertaking. Ray could cover content and Albert could cover the video production. Ray would host the show and students would present news, weather, teen alerts, etc.

They pooled their money and created a 45-minute pilot video with all the bells and whistles, which cost them about $75,000. The pilot was fabulous—just what they had hoped to present to get the funding they needed to create a regular show for high school students across the nation.

However, Ray and Albert could not market the program. After the initial excitement began to fade, they floundered. Many of those who saw it seemed interested at first, but when it came time to back it financially, the people they had expected would be sponsors got cold feet.

The clock was ticking and Ray and Albert were not getting results. They spent a considerable amount of savings and got no results. The partnership wavered and misunderstandings abounded. Neither was considered the leader by the other.

In time, these two best friends became enemies. Since they had never drawn up a partnership agreement, no commitment remained to bind them together. Each felt ripped off by the other. Failure tore them apart and brought out the worst in them. To this day, Albert and Ray do not talk.

Analysis

Where did Albert and Ray go wrong?

Why didn't their idea catch on?

Why didn't Albert and Ray get the financial sponsorship they needed to succeed?

Ray started out as an educator and Albert as a video producer. Neither was a business type, and they were not marketing oriented. It never occurred to them that the world would *not* be crazy for their idea and would *not* jump behind them in enthusiastic support. Ray knew books and assumed he understood the video aspect of the education business. This was not the case.

Ray and Albert never understood where their market was and who it was made up of. The only thing they had known about their audience was that it was high school students. All else was assumption. They based their business on these assumptions, which became their downfall. They never discovered their market. Neither served in the role of leader/CEO. Both were acting like vice presidents. Their ship went way off course as a result.

Lessons to Be Learned

To create a successful business, the tremendous enthusiasm generated by idea people like Ray and Albert needs to be harnessed and made practical. Instead, Ray and Albert fell in love with their own idea. That was the beginning of the end. They never checked to see what the market potential was for the video series or how complicated it might be to market.

It is hard to give up on a good idea once it bites you; Ray and Albert were bitten. They never looked back. As a result, there was a one in a million chance that the video would have caught on. Unless you research your market and project sales realistically, your chances are equally as low. Can you afford to take these kind of chances? When the pressure is on, someone has to step up and be the leader. Ray and Albert lacked the entrepreneurial skills required for success.

 Your Turn   *Answer the following questions:*

- ► If you are forming a partnership, are you aware of each individual's shortcomings?

- ► Do you and your partner have a commitment to specific goals and shared visions?

See also *Managing Disagreement Constructively,* by Herbert S. Kindler, Ph.D., Crisp Publications; *Starting Your New Business: A Guide for Entrepreneurs,* by Charles L. Martin, Ph.D., Crisp Publications; *Writing and Implementing a Marketing Plan,* by Richard F. Gerson, Ph.D., Crisp Publications.

CASE STUDY

The Missing Quality Controls

Small businesses, especially start-up businesses that may not know their clients well, must continually test their assumptions about how well they are serving those clients. They need to talk with clients periodically or build a follow-up program that gives clients the opportunity to complain. Every complaint provides an opportunity to satisfy a customer.

In this case study, Dave learned the hard way how important it is to stay in touch with his customers.

When Dave graduated from the local junior college, he immediately went to work for a small company that sold and installed telephone systems. Over the next ten years, he participated in nearly every part of the company and learned every aspect of the business—selling, installing and servicing. The thing he learned best was that the owners—not the employees—make the big money.

He decided to start his own company. For the next three years, Dave sold systems to businesses of all sizes. He hired business associates to help him install and service his clients. As Dave's business continued to grow, he realized that he would either have to hire office staff or shift some of his business to outside firms.

After learning about the administrative paperwork and incredible expenses associated with hiring and maintaining staff, Dave decided to farm out the installation and service components of his business to one of his friends who had started another small business.

Dave concentrated on designing and selling telephone systems. Despite a poor economy, his revenues grew over the next two years. However, he began to notice that his early clients were no longer returning his calls. When he did speak with them, they were abrupt and appeared disinterested in further conversation. Clients' responses to direct mail offer specials began to have the same response rates as direct mail to companies he had not previously contacted and those he had not previously done business with.

Recognizing that something was wrong, Dave made luncheon appointments with some of his earliest clients to find out what had caused the shift of allegiance in his trusted client base. What he heard during those meetings opened Dave's eyes.

The director of a trade association told Dave a horror story of having had limited telephone service for nearly two days before his problem was fixed. The director of marketing at a law firm told Dave that the firm had to wait three days beyond a planned rearranging of their offices to get their telephones moved. Another client indicated that when his company had called for routine servicing for some of the phones, the technician had taken several days to come out, rather than the usual one-day service that Dave had provided.

Analysis

What was going wrong?

Why were Dave's customers no longer interested in doing business with him?

What was Dave's mistake?

Dave was good at design and sales. He even called every client after installation to make certain everything went well and that they were happy with their new telephone systems. He failed, however, to maintain quality control over all aspects of his business.

To reduce his workload and grow the company, Dave placed customer service outside of his direct control. It was a while before he found out that the company providing his installation and service was killing his repeat sales opportunities. He did not know until, in some cases, it was too late. He had not established a quality control mechanism to let him know when there were complaints.

Dave needed to get himself back into the communications loop with all his customers—whether or not he personally handles service calls. He had several options. For example, he could have required the service technicians to leave a quality assurance postcard with each client. Addressed to Dave at his sales office, Dave would have an opportunity to monitor and influence the level of customer service.

Lessons to Be Learned

You cannot afford even one unhappy customer. To remove the potential of poor customer service from your business environment, you need to build a feedback loop that will let you know what is going on all of the time. It takes too much energy to get a customer, to lose one so easily.

Your Turn   *Answer the following questions:*

► Are your customers happy with your service?

► Do you have a customer feedback system in place?

See also *Quality Customer Service,* by William B. Martin, Ph.D., Crisp Publications; *Managing Quality Customer Service,* by William B. Martin, Ph.D., Crisp Publications

CASE STUDY

Hot for a Franchise at any Price

You need to know exactly what you are getting into when you start a business. This means that you must fully understand the field you are entering and must not, for example, rely solely on a franchisor's judgement. Change is constant in business; if your franchisor had misread the market, you will most certainly suffer.

In this case study, Bob made the mistake of relying exclusively on a franchisor's view. He did not use his entrepreneurial instincts.

After he graduated from a major university, Bob had a successful career in the military. He planned to retire after thirty years of service and go into business for himself. To prepare, before he retired he took as many courses as he could in management, small business planning and financial management. He enjoyed the courses, which got him more excited about having his own business.

After he assessed all the ways to go into business, Bob decided to buy a franchise. He was convinced that the advantages of buying a franchise outweighed the additional expenses associated with franchising fees, and plunked down his $150,000 for a quick printing business. In no time, assisted by his franchisor, Bob was in business. His vision of the business—to do a lot of quick printing and copying work—was dictated by the franchisor.

Bob suddenly found that there were thirty printers in his immediate business district alone. Many of these franchises were quite similar to Bob's. His business got off to a slow start because of this competition among printing franchises.

Besides the heavy competition, technology was revolutionizing the printing business. Bob found out the hard way that his franchise package did not come with the current quick printing technology when he saw that his competitors had an advantage of being able to serve customers more cheaply and faster.

Bob struggled, putting in long hours to get business and remain competitive. He hired two people to help with the copying and printing and another person to work the retail desk. Still, he found more printing franchises opening nearby that were very high tech and far more competitive than Bob could be. He was just getting by.

Bob's disappointment got the best of him, since his expectations for a successful franchise business were not being met. He become increasingly discouraged and considered selling his franchise.

Analysis

Where did Bob start to go wrong?

Did Bob really understand the printing business?

What can Bob do to turn around his quick printing franchise?

When you buy a franchise, you let the franchisor determine the viability of the business potential. Bob had the capital to invest and he was looking for a business opportunity. In fact, the money was burning a hole in his pocket. He let the franchisor convince him that the printing business would be profitable. Without doing his own research, Bob had no idea just how competitive the market was until after he made his purchase.

The market was changing rapidly around him and his franchise; new technology was quickly changing the way business was done. Bob did not notice until it was too late. His demise was due, in part, to his lack of awareness and understanding of the business that he was getting into.

Turnaround would be a long shot, since Bob would need to purchase technological equipment to be more competitive. He would have to dig into his pockets or find and investor who was willing to take a considerable risk.

Lessons to Be Learned

Before you decide on a business, make certain you have done solid market research and have determined exactly what is going on in your particular market. Markets vary from city to city; what is true in one market may not be true for another. Bob did not check out his market thoroughly enough. If he had, he would have been much more familiar with the printing business and prepared for his competition. The entrepreneur knows exactly what is at risk at all times and what it takes to be successful.

Answer the following questions:

> ► Have you done your own market research or are you relying on someone else's opinion?

> ► List five advantages you have over your competition.

    1.

    2.

    3.

    4.

    5.

See also *Risk Taking,* by Herbert S. Kindler, Ph.D., Crisp Publications; *Starting Your New Business: A Guide for Entrepreneurs,* by Charles L. Martin, Ph.D., Crisp Publications; *Buying Your First Franchise,* by Elwood N. Chapman, Crisp Publications.

CASE STUDY

No Direction, No Results

Entrepreneurs need to have more than great ideas. They cannot get distracted by yet another great possibility until they are assured that their current great idea has become a financial success. They need to have follow-through, the ability to create financial success, and subsequently be able to harvest the profits.

In this case study, Jim made the mistake of diluting his success by following too many of his great ideas. Individuals who work for large corporations and have been rewarded for their innovative ideas often behave like Jim when they strike out on their own.

Out of the many high-technology firms that tried to recruit him when he graduated cum laude in electrical engineering from a prestigious university, Jim chose to join a blue-chip firm. For more than twenty years he climbed the corporate ladder; when he left, he was head of data processing for a large and profitable division, and he was considered one of the best upper-middle-level managers—the type that corporations hate to lose.

For a long time, Jim had felt the itch to start his own business. He was intrigued by the many success stories he had heard, and he dreamed of the day that he would be able to tell his success story. He had prepared himself by taking courses in small business management at the local college. Since he enjoyed meeting small business principals at the events sponsored by the local Chamber of Commerce, he had also done a considerable amount of networking.

After several years of preparation, Jim launched his computer software firm. Convinced they could benefit by becoming computerized, he wanted to provide services to small businesses. So he promoted his services to small businesses and he was very enthusiastic about his modest results. However, although he was making enough to pay the bills, Jim came to the realization that small business principals were a very hard sell; since there was a considerable investment for them, they had to be absolutely convinced of the value of computerization.

Jim also became interested in very specialized computer programming that examined population data and its implications for businesses. All this data was tied to government census information that required special computer equipment. Jim purchased the equipment and began to market the specialty service to retailers, since the information provided by the service could prove invaluable to retailers who are selecting locations.

Jim's time and energy began to be stretched between the two different marketing plans he was following and markets he was pursuing. This was a monumental task for a beginner. Not surprisingly, since his marketing time was split between the two, he was not generating results in either area.

Jim then became interested in some innovative personal computing telecommunications hardware. He contacted the manufacturer and, after some training, he became the local representative. He was very excited over the possibilities of selling the hardware, convinced that small businesses would benefit greatly.

Jim began to call on prospects, trying to sell them on the idea that buying this hardware was like adding a staff member who could answer the phone and give and take critical information. Within a couple of months, when his cash flow became a serious problem, Jim realized that the sales cycle from the first call to the sale was much longer than he had calculated.

Jim was preoccupied with selling the telecommunications equipment. Meanwhile, Jim had neglected his other two services: his computerization consultancy, which was yielding few, if any, leads, was failing; the census data information service was also producing almost no business.

Jim was not getting results from any of his business efforts. He was having more and more trouble paying his bills. His enthusiasm did not produce business and his financial problems continued to mount until Jim could no longer go on.

Analysis

What was Jim's mistake?

What could Jim have done to create success?

What good did it do for Jim to have so many interests?

Jim could not focus. The moment he got something going, he became distracted by a new interest that he would pursue. He was opportunistic to a fault, and he saw possibilities for any number of business opportunities. But he never stuck with one long enough to make it successful. Staying focused is a classic characteristic of successful entrepreneurs.

It is a wonderful attribute to discover all kinds of business interests and to be able to see the possibilities for business success. However, when you take this to extremes, you are faced with the plight of the Jims of the business world.

Lessons to Be Learned

Jim's story is not unique. It is a classic example of what happens to many small business entrepreneurs. As a CEO, you have to be able direct your company with a vision that will get you into a position of success. To be a successful entrepreneur, you have to produce the results that will not only keep you in business, but that will grow your business.

Your Turn

Answer the following questions:

► Can you focus on a business possibility and make it financially successful?

► Do you have a vision for your business that guides you each and every day?

► Are you able to fight off distractions that can pull you away from your vision?

See also *Goals and Goal Setting,* by Larrie Rouillard, Crisp Publications; *Consulting For Success: A Practical Guide for Prospective Consultants,* by David Karlson, Ph.D., Crisp Publications.

CASE STUDY

Vision Without Verification

Assumptions about important business decisions are some of the most frequent mistakes made. Newcomers to business get sold on their own ideas for businesses and proceed without determining demand. And when they are sold on something, they cannot usually be dissuaded from pursuing the business ventures full steam.

This "go with your gut" reaction or "follow your instincts" mentality can lead to success if you do some simple research to make sure the idea is viable. In this case study, Judy suffered the consequences of not doing that necessary research.

Judy's background was in public relations and fund raising. Over a fifteen-year period, she had worked for many different organizations and had been very successful in all her assignments.

During the last ten years, she had done fund raising, principally for nonprofit organizations (churches, Red Cross, etc.). She had become very good at raising money by conducting large special events that were co-sponsored by large for-profit corporations as well as the nonprofit organization that was her employer. For example, a large retailer would host a fundraiser at its store and donate all proceeds to the Red Cross.

The only difficulty she found in fund raising was working with boards of directors who wanted to micro-manage her successful events. And, she felt that she deserved a larger financial return for the results she was delivering, since she was paid a straight salary, regardless of the success of her work.

She decided to establish a fund-raising firm in her rural community. Judy's envisioned herself being a top fund raiser for the types of nonprofit organizations that she had worked for over the years. She had a great track record and was convinced that there was a market for her services, especially since the results she achieved contributed directly to the organizations' bottom lines.

It was not long before Judy's vision for a successful consulting firm in a rural community became questionable. No one in her part of the country was hiring independent fund-raising consultants. None of the prospective nonprofit organizations were willing to work on a percentage basis, that is, sharing with Judy a portion of the funds raised as a result of her services. Nor were they willing to pay an up-front fee for her services.

They wanted a staff member on their staff who would do fund raising for a salary that was far less than what Judy was asking. The nonprofit organizations were successful as they had been operating, so they had no incentive to change the way they raised money.

Judy's prospective market did not want to pay for her services. Very disappointed, she was soon forced to withdraw her vision for a private fund-raising consulting firm. This was a considerable loss to her, since she had put so much of her energy into the idea and had spent considerable capital marketing it.

Analysis

Where did Judy go wrong?

What could Judy have done to avoid her mistake?

Why does it take more than a dream to be successful?

As an inside staff member who was very successful, Judy did not yet feel she was receiving the monetary recognition she deserved. In addition, she was treated more like a volunteer than as a valued professional. This is a classic pattern in nonprofit organizations that use a lot of volunteers to do the work of the organization.

Judy started her firm out of her frustration and anger. She assumed that nonprofits would pay for professional consultant fund raising services. Neither the percentage approach nor the fee approach was acceptable, because nonprofit organizations in her part of the country do not conduct business that way.

Convinced she had the idea—a vision for a service that would be in demand—and sure that it would be successful, Judy quit her job. Her biggest mistake was not checking out the demand for the service. She was so sold on the idea that she did not consult with prospective clients to see if they agreed. This mistake proved fatal. Entrepreneurs minimize risk by becoming keenly aware of their business ideas potential for success.

Lessons to Be Learned

Newcomers to business are often afraid someone is going to steal their great idea. Their anxiety to get going blinds them from pausing to check that their great ideas are practical—that is, will prospects pay for their services? Be sure that you are not so anxious to get started that you overlook the realities of your market. Make sure you have an audience that is receptive to your products and services before you risk more than you can afford to lose.

Your Turn

Answer the following questions:

► Are you sure there is a market for your idea?

► List five things you have done (or you will do) to be sure there will be buyers for what you are selling?

1.

2.

3.

4.

5.

See also *Operating A Really Small Business,* by Betty Bivins, Crisp Publications.

CASE STUDY

Diversifying Too Soon

When business principals succeed in one business, they often think they can succeed easily in another. They reason that since big corporations diversify, it must be the thing to do.

Diversifying does not always lead to success, you will see when you read this case study.

David had a white collar, technical background. He had held technical support positions in high-technology companies after earning his degree in electrical engineering. David's outside interests included woodworking and in the evenings he pursued a degree in business at the local university.

David liked to design and make furniture that was unique and functional, and he was quite good at it. His designs, as well as the quality of his furniture, got him rave reviews. Sally, David's wife, was also his number-one admirer of the furniture he made for their home.

After David finished his degree in business, he decided to start his own boutique and furniture-manufacturing business. He targeted the young professional market that wanted the basics in furniture for the bedroom. David designed several styles of platform beds, hide-a-beds, bedside tables and chests of drawers. Sally learned everything there was to know about manufacturing futon mattresses, which were the rage at the time.

David and Sally saved and invested in enough equipment to produce the furniture and mattresses. They leased some very inexpensive warehouse space in the remote suburbs that included a showroom store front. They could afford the space and counted on customers traveling to their location to see the finely crafted furniture that they priced to fit the young professionals' budgets.

The couple promoted their new venture with a tiny advertisement for their classic, all-oak hide-a-bed sofa that they ran each Friday in the metropolitan area's major newspaper home section. They positioned this product as their "flagship" and priced it below all competitors. Their plan was to sell volumes of this piece so that they could realize economies and efficiency in manufacturing, which would ensure them a profit.

They had positioned themselves correctly. Every Saturday, the little showroom was filled with customers who bought like crazy. The young professionals loved the functional designs and liked buying at such a fair price from a local craftsman. David and Sally added manufacturing staff in the first year, and in the second and third years volume and profits grew steadily.

During the fourth year, they opened two showrooms in the city. The showrooms got good traffic, but the full-time staff they required raised overhead dramatically. Profits began to decline as competition heated up, especially in the platform bed line that had become David and Sally's main product line.

That same year, David and Sally—who had three young children—become interested in children's clothing. They had noticed that children's clothing was very expensive and of marginal quality. Sally became obsessed with the idea of going into the children's clothing business. She explored endlessly the sources of high quality children's clothes.

The couple became so preoccupied with the children's clothing business opportunity that they stopped paying close attention to their furniture business. They did not notice that profits from their main product line, which had been so successful, was steadily slipping.

They decided to diversify and go into children's clothing and ordered thousands of dollars of inventory from a source for children's clothes they found in Scandinavia. They leased costly space that was a sure winner in a highly desirable location in town. Wanting to convey an upscale quality image, they invested a considerable sum to decorate the clothes store.

As it turned out, a giant children's toy retailer and other business owners had seen the need for quality children's clothes at just about the same time as David and Sally. Overnight, the field was crowded with competitors jumping into the children's clothing market. The baby boom was in full swing and there was money to be made.

Their children's clothes store got off to a good start. But the volume necessary to cover all the overhead, coupled with the narrow mark-ups they could charge, left them at break-even at best. Their overhead was eating them alive.

At the same time, the profits from the furniture operation began to shrink due to competition. And, since they were so preoccupied with the children's clothes store, they were not paying enough attention to the furniture business.

Within a few months, they found themselves in over their heads. The volume was not there to sustain either business. David and Sally were forced to dig into their savings to keep the businesses afloat. For the first time they realized that they were in deep trouble, and they did not see a way out.

Analysis

What went wrong for David and Sally? When did it go wrong?

How smart is it to diversify?

What could David and Sally have done to avoid business failure?

David and Sally made the mistake of not fully maximizing their growth in the furniture business. They could have done much more business in furniture, but did not want to spend the money that would be needed to aggressively market the handcrafted local furniture plant and all its fine products. Instead, they were distracted with a retail clothing business—a whole other world when it comes to doing business successfully.

If they had stuck to what they knew well, they would have had a much greater opportunity to remain competitive. By the time they realized what was happening in the furniture business, it was too late to recover. Competition that heavily affected their thriving business had moved in.

Diversifying is certainly one way to grow the business. But you have to know the business you are getting into. Furniture manufacturing is very different from the retail children's clothing business. David and Sally got in over their heads and they paid for it dearly. In the end, they lost both businesses.

Lessons to Be Learned

David and Sally lost their vision for their furniture business. They let their early success mislead them into thinking that they could do another terrific start-up business in another market. It is not that easy.

If you re-examine your vision and see where you want to go, there are usually tremendous opportunities to grow the business you are in. David and Sally had a furniture plant and were making only bedroom furniture. They had never even explored the furniture manufacturing possibilities for the other rooms in a house!

Your Turn   *Answer the following questions:*

► Have you carefully examined your current business to see what other products and services you might offer?

► List four things you might do to expand your current business.

1.

2.

3.

4.

See also *Managing The Family Business,* by Marshall Northington, Ph.D., Crisp Publications; *Marketing Strategies for Small Businesses,* by Richard F. Gerson, Ph.D., Crisp Publications.

ASK YOURSELF

► Describe the market you are trying to enter.

► Discuss the impact of competition in your market. Include the potential effect(s) of technology on your business.

► What is your vision of your successful business? How do you plan to prove it is worth pursuing?

CHAPTER
FIVE

FINANCIAL
MISTAKES

FINANCIALS ARE OFTEN A MYSTERY

Many people who own small businesses have very little background in the financial aspects of running those businesses. Typically, they have been involved previously with the delivery of the goods or services that they now are trying to establish as business enterprise. They may have been engineers, staffers or mechanics—they have usually worked, as employees, in other businesses.

When new business owners go into business for themselves, financials are frequently something of a mystery to them. Those who have limited experience in this important area often make mistakes that impair any possibilities of their growing successful businesses.

The financial mistakes that follow are some those made most commonly. Of course, both novice business owners and seasoned veterans make many more financial mistakes than those represented by these examples.

To succeed in your own business, you must understand the financials. The figures tell the story.

CASE STUDY

Lease or Buy?

If you do not commit to your business, you may not get a chance to fully compete in the market. Commitment takes time, energy and finances. Many business people hold back on one or more of these essential resources. Too late, they wonder why success has passed them by.

In this case study, Mark was lucky. Before it was too late, he realized the total commitment he needed to make. If you want to succeed, make sure you know where your market is going and be sure you are committed—in time, energy and finances—to meet the needs of your customers.

Mark had been a well-known and successful country club golf pro. For ten years he ran the country club pro shop and provided golf instruction to the members. He always knew that there was a limit on what he could make as a club pro, so he explored all the business possibilities directly associated with golf.

Although Mark determined that his best bet for developing greater financial return was to open a driving range, he was unsure about the popularity of golf. Therefore, he leased the ten acres he required for the driving range on a yearly basis.

Over the years, Mark and his landlord developed a stormy relationship. As a result, Mark's never knew if he would have a lease until just before the next golf season began. This led him to run his business on a year-to-year basis, with no plans for real growth and change. Since his investment could be lost at the end of the year, he could not even consider making basic improvements such as better tees, all weather shelter, etc. And, since his parcel was only sized for a driving range, he could not add services such as batting cages for softball and baseball.

Twenty-seven years passed. Other than earning a reputation of running a good driving range, Mark was not much better off than when he started his business. In those twenty-seven years, golf became more popular and the competition grew. His competitors were investing in their ranges, converting them to year-round activities, with enclosed, heated tee areas and adding video golf instruction, batting cages, pitch and putt, and retail pro shops with all the latest in golfing gear and apparel.

Mark had no way to grow his business like his competitors. Since he could not count on having a lease for the next season, he could not invest in his leased situation. In spite of his many years of good service, he was rapidly losing ground to his competition.

He finally realized that the only way he could succeed was to acquire land. Since he had been prudent during the 27 years he had been in business, he was able to invest in a 20-acre parcel of land that, miraculously, become available near the range where he leased and was so well known.

The rest is history. Mark developed a premier driving range and golf center. The business is now run by his two sons. One is waiting to join the pro tour as soon as he learns the family business.

Analysis

What was Mark's mistake in judgment?

Why did it take Mark so long to respond?

Mark did not think long-term. It was not his nature; he was more comfortable putting up with a difficult landlord, on a year-to-year basis for 27 years. He was a golf pro, not a businessman.

However, when he realized that the future of his business was contingent on his taking a risk by investing in his business, he became a businessman. And, he became a very successful one.

Since his range was located in a seasonal climate area where golf is not played year round, Mark had been caught up in the seasonal nature of his activity. In the early years, without major competition and with the seasonal nature of golf at that time, his business was less affected by Mark's short-term planning. Later, with the steady growth in popularity of golf, he had the opportunity to respond to his customers' needs. He made a financial investment in the land he acquired, which gave him a second chance to make it on his own.

Lessons to Be Learned

To be successful, you must be committed to your business, have faith in your judgment, and jump in when the time is right.

Mark was fortunate; it was only a matter of time before Mark's competitors would have "driven" him out of business. He had successfully avoided jumping in and making his financial commitment for 27 years, and he saw the light in time to become a serious competitor in the sports business.

Today, Mark is in the entertainment business associated with the game of golf. It is a place where families gather, with an ice cream parlor, a miniature golf course, a year-round driving range, a pro shop with golf apparel and a wide selection of clubs, and golf lessons taught by a PGA professional. Mark has even more planned.

Your Turn

Answer the following questions:

► Are you fully committed to your business?

► Do you have a plan for expanding your business?

► List five things that are in the way of your business expanding.

1.

2.

3.

4.

5.

See also *Financial Analysis: The Next Step,* by James O. Gill, Crisp Publications; *Starting Your New Business: A Guide for Entrepreneurs,* by Charles L. Martin, Ph.D., Crisp Publications.

CASE STUDY

Fire Sale—Giving Your Services Away

Pricing yourself low is not usually a recommended practice, but sometimes it can help you establish your track record. However, if you quote too low, prospects become suspicious of the quality they can expect. There is a fine line between setting fees too high and too low. Walk it carefully.

In this case study, Sarah made the mistake of setting her fees too low. Notice the ramifications so you can avoid repeating Sarah's mistake.

Sarah had been a successful fund raiser for many years. She was an astute writer with a record of producing top-notch proposals, that substantially improved the chances of her projects being funded.

Like many professionals who work within organizations, Sarah yearned for the freedom and the financial return that come with having your own firm. She also wanted greater control of her time, so she could give her children the attention they wanted and spend less on child care.

Her solution was to open a consulting firm that provided grant-writing services to organizations that were seeking funding from foundations. She based her fees on writing simple grants that she knew she could knock out within eight hours.

Sarah quickly became known as the low-cost grant writer, and did not have to advertise because word-of-mouth referrals brought her the clients she needed. In many cases, after she wrote a grant for one department in an organization, several other departments in the same organization would use her services.

When Sarah examined her financial posture, she found that she was making about the same amount of money that she had made when she was working as a full time employee. She had thought that she would have more income working for herself, especially since she was so busy.

When she carefully analyzed her quotation proposals, Sarah found that she was giving away business, especially considering the value of her services and her success rate in getting proposals funded. She realized that she was a bargain when it came to doing a simple proposal. For example, the simple proposals that Sarah could write in eight hours would take the junior fund raiser in a company days to write. She also undercut her daily basic proposal rate when she felt strongly about the cause she was working for.

The children were unhappy because she was so busy that she also had less time for them. Even though mom was at home, she could not be bothered because she had important grants to write.

Early on, her husband had supported her bringing her business into the house; now he questioned Sarah about her goals. Sarah began to seriously question her decision to go into business for herself. She was extremely unhappy with her situation.

Analysis

Where did Sarah's business get out of control when it came to making the kind of money she deserved?

What was Sarah doing wrong?

How could Sarah turn around her situation?

From the outset, Sarah undervalued her services and undercharged her clients. She had been under the misconception that, because it was so simple for her to write a grant, her product was not worth the money she should have charged.

As a result, she had all the takers she could handle. Her profit margin was too low for the quality of work she was producing. So she had to take in a high volume of work to make the same amount of money she had made working full time. Under this financial set-up, Sarah could not get ahead. In fact, she was getting behind—especially when she severely undercharged many of her clients for grants that were for causes she believed in.

To satisfy herself and her family, Sarah needed to reconsider the value of her services. Typical of many new independent professionals when they first go into business, Sarah was insecure and undervalued her services. Afraid to charge more, she feared that prospective clients would not hire her.

Sarah will have to use her track record to prove her value to prospects, because she needs to increase her prices. She can do this in relation to the results that she can promise.

Sarah was worth her daily basic fee and much, much more. Without knowing it, she gave away her services for the first year. Then she discovered just how little money she had made.

Lessons to Be Learned

At first, underpricing services can give a new business owner an opportunity to demonstrate his or her capabilities. He or she has a chance to acquire a major track record.

At some point, however, that business owner needs to think like a business person, valuing his or her services in relation to the results created by those services. The business person attaches a fair dollar value to the combination of services and results.

Setting fees is very tricky for newcomers to business who have been on fixed, predictable salaries. Having to shift gears and think of the business financials is especially difficult. To determine a fair pricing structure, consider the prevailing market rate, the individual's experience, and what he or she can prove to deliver. Set your fees carefully; if you set them too low, you could find yourself in Sarah's situation; if you set them to high, no one will use you.

Once you set your fees, it is a good idea to project what you can expect to make in best- and worst-case scenarios. Then you will not have any surprises at the end of the year.

Your Turn

Answer the following questions:

▶ What is the fair market value of your products/services?

▶ What are the prevailing market rates for your products/ services?

▶ What yearly income have you projected from your fees?

See also *Consulting for Success: A Practical Guide for Prospective Consultants*, by David Karlson, Ph.D., Crisp Publications; *The Basics of Budgeting*, by Terry Dickey, Crisp Publications.

CASE STUDY

Payroll is Eating Up All the Profits!

When owners of successful start-up companies want to change their basic services, they need to be sure they understand the nature of the new services.

In this case study, Frank's decision to change the services of his franchise met with near-disaster.

Frank and his father, Fred, run a successful muffler-replacement franchise. In fact, Fred was a legend when it came to the volume of business generated from his first shop.

He had picked the perfect location for the first store, having concluded that site was everything when it came to a shop's location. He had located the business in the middle of sixteen car dealerships and right on the main highway. Since the car dealerships generated so much business in new and used cars, and in service, the traffic was great. With good signs, Fred's and Frank's muffler franchise was the top producer in the country.

Over the next five years, Fred and Frank opened many more shops, with relative success. As other muffler franchises entered the market, the competition grew. This, of course, decreased the volume of their business, especially at their newer locations. To beat the competition, Frank and Fred decided to offer more services.

The most logical to them was to offer brake replacement. They planned to offer brakes at their newest shop, which Frank had started. Frank realized they would need a more highly trained staff to support this new service. He studied the labor market and competition, and determined that they would have to pay much higher hourly wages to offer brake services.

Fred thought the wages for brake services were too high, but Frank went ahead and offered the new mechanics the substantially higher hourly rate plus a percentage of the sales.

Frank and Fred had positioned their shop to be the budgetary choice for brake replacement, and were now paying cadillac wages. After several months, Frank realized that the amount they were paying to the new brake/muffler mechanics was eating them alive. By the end of the year, the shop was in the red and had to be carried by their successful shops. Frank was upset, having pushed so hard for the new service at any cost. Although he knew the muffler business, the brake business had fooled him.

Analysis

What went wrong for Frank?

What was Frank's mistake?

Frank and Fred had decided that they wanted to be a low-cost/high-quality brake and muffler shop. Since Frank did not project the bottom-line impact of the higher wages he thought he had to pay to brake mechanics, he was being eaten alive with higher costs/overhead.

Later, after doing more research, he learned that the percentage of sales he was giving to the mechanics was also too high. Frank had lost site of the fact that once he hired the new employees, he was faced with a fixed cost for employees that he could not afford.

Since their competitors had the same idea about expanding market share by offering additional services, the brake business did not get off to a rapid start. What seemed like a great idea got the experimental shop into deep trouble when it had to be underwritten by their other "mufflers only" stores.

Frank could have avoided his mistake by checking more thoroughly on the wages of qualified mechanics. He was not thorough and he did not project the impact at the bottom line.

Lessons to Be Learned

Thoroughness is key in business and avoiding assumptions is critical. Frank had assumed that he would have to pay a lot more for mechanics; however, he paid beyond the capability of revenues he generated. To continue with the business as he had set it up, he would be forced to charge higher prices and reposition the brake business as a high-quality, high-cost service.

Your Turn   *Answer the following questions:*

► Have you realistically projected your personnel expenses against the income you will generate?

► Do you understand all aspects of the new services you might offer?

See also *Starting Your New Business: A Guide for Entrepreneurs*, by Charles L. Martin, Ph.D., Crisp Publications; *Employee Benefits with Cost Control*, by Rebecca R. Luhn, Ph.D., Crisp Publications.

CASE STUDY

The Check Is in the Mail!

Most new business firms and sole practitioners do not realize that getting and doing the work are one part of the business equation; getting paid is a totally separate part.

In this case study, Rick learned by bitter lesson how important it is to establish a workable pay schedule.

Rick had graduated cum laude from a prestigious university, with a degree in chemical engineering. After he completed his MBA, he was recruited by a large chemical corporation. For the next twenty-five years he climbed the corporate ladder and achieved a reputation of being a top producer on every assignment.

However, Rick lacked political savvy. In fact, he fell out of favor because he was unable to gain political support. Subsequently, he was farmed out from corporate headquarters to head up a losing specialty automobile plastics chemical factory. The factory was a poor acquisition that the company had acquired in the company's expansionist days and had never lived up to its expectations. Rick was given the impossible task of turning the factory around. He labored for several years before the corporation closed the facility. That was when they presented Rick with his pink slip.

Rick stewed for several months before he decided to try his hand at consulting. He had a lot of contacts in the field and thought that consulting would be right up his ally. Unfortunately, terrible economic times arrived at the same time; the corporations in Rick's network were laying off full-time employees and were not hiring consultants.

While watching his severance pay rapidly disappear, Rick became increasingly hungry for work—any work. He was entering the financial danger zone: his monthly mortgage payments were becoming nearly impossible to make; college tuition for both of his daughters was due in two months.

During his networking, Rick met Joe, an established consultant. Joe had acquired a management consulting contract that he needed some help fulfilling. He offered Rick a couple of weeks of work, out of town, in which he could earn a generous daily fee and all his expenses would be paid. Rick was ecstatic over his good fortune. He accepted the assignment on a handshake.

The next week, Rick began his out of town subcontractor assignment. After a week, he realized that he had not clarified how his expenses would be reimbursed. So Rick called Joe, who confirmed that all expenses would be reimbursed. Joe asked Rick to cover all his expenses, including food, hotel, mileage, etc., for the next two weeks.

This seemed reasonable to Rick, who put all his expense on his American Express Card. Within two weeks, Rick had accumulated daily expenses of $150, for a two-week total of $2,000, plus transportation expenses. Rick assumed he would be reimbursed within thirty days, and that he would be able to pay his American Express bill, which is due upon receipt.

Near the end of the second week of the assignment, Joe called to tell Rick that the contract had been extended. Rick was thrilled when he heard he was to have two more weeks of work. When he asked Joe when he would be reimbursed for his expenses and receive his consulting fees, Joe complained about a cash-flow problem. Joe told Rick that he would be paid as soon as the client paid, which would be any day.

The next two weeks passed and Rick's expenses grew by another $2,000, plus, for a total of $5,000. He continued to charge all his expenses on his American Express card.

Rick completed the assignment and returned home. He was pleased with the consulting assignment, but had not received a penny toward his expenses or his consulting fees.

He checked in with Joe, who congratulated him on a job well done. Knowing that Rick was new to the consulting field and needed to build his reputation as a effective consultant, Joe volunteered to be a reference for Rick.

Then Rick asked about his expense money. Joe said he expected to be reimbursed by the client in thirty days; Rick would have to wait until after that, since Joe was having a cash-flow problem and could not cover Rick's expenses until he was reimbursed. And Rick would also get his consulting fees in thirty days.

Rick explained his financial crunch to Joe, but got no satisfaction. Rick was extremely disheartened. Joe's cash-flow problems had become Rick's. Joe owed him expenses and fees in excess of $27,000, which he did not pay until ninety days after Rick completed his assignment.

Before Joe had paid Rick, the damage to Rick's credit had been done. American Express restricted Rick's credit card privileges. Rick's other creditors reported Rick to the credit bureau, which resulted in a black mark on Rick's credit rating. Since Rick was two months behind in his mortgage payments, his home mortgage banker threatened foreclosure.

Analysis

What went wrong?

Where did Rick make a mistake?

A classic mistake, Rick allowed himself to be manipulated into covering his expenses up-front when he could ill-afford to take on more debt. In his excitement about the work, he did not think about who, what and when he would be paid.

Rick should have gotten clarity on the financial arrangements of the assignment when he and Joe first spoke. Instead, Rick agreed to do the work without establishing terms. The terms should have included when he would be paid, who would cover expenses, and how those expenses would be covered.

While Rick was clearly naive, Joe allowed him to over-extend himself, knowing that Rick would not be paid until the client paid Joe. Joe was looking out for himself; Rick was not. Rick needed to clarify expenses from the outset. He should have either received an advance for expenses, or set up direct billing for his expenses to Joe's company.

Rick should have also negotiated terms of payment for his fees. He might have negotiated for payment in advance or payment every two weeks. By bringing up the issue, Rick could have negotiated reasonably with Joe, sensitizing Joe to his needs—especially his mortgage. Joe had no idea of Rick's financial problems, and Rick was too proud to bring up the subject. After all he had been a successful corporate executive!

Lessons to Be Learned

Most start-up business owners do not know how or when to ask for payment. They simply do not realize how long it can take to get paid. Beware—it always takes longer than you think.

Payment is out of your control unless you make advance agreements. Even then, you cannot be sure. When you are hungry, it is easier to take on assignments without thinking of the outcome—especially payment.

Be sure you ask, "When do I get paid?" or "How do I get paid?" And remember, your creditors have their terms of payment spelled out clearly. If you do not clarify your payment terms, you will look naive and inexperienced. Business persons are expected to raise terms of payment, up front, as the deals are being made—not afterwards, when there is little leverage.

Your Turn   *Answer the following questions:*

► How long will it take you to collect your accounts receivables?

► Do you negotiate payment terms up front with your clients?

See also *Successful Negotiation*, by Robert Maddux, Crisp Publications; *Consulting for Success: A Practical Guide for Prospective Consultants*, by David Karlson, Ph.D., Crisp Publications; *Marketing Your Consulting or Professional Services*, by David Karlson, Ph.D., Crisp Publications.

CASE STUDY

No Money for Promotion Means No Growth!

Be patient and invest your scarce capital wisely on only those items that will bring immediate returns. Too many times, new business owners assume that they must have it all.

In this case study, Harry invested far more than was prudent for his business. The results were disheartening and, potentially, financially disastrous.

Harry is a very creative person who tends to act on his intuition. He earned a master's degree from a very prestigious graphic design school and had been very successful as a graphics designer, commanding a six-figure income.

For years Harry had dreamed of starting a quick printing business that combined graphic design and printing under one roof. His instincts had guided every decision Harry made, and this business idea was no exception. Since he had so much experience with printers as a customer, Harry thought he knew a lot about what it would take to run a printing business.

Convinced that he could make a very special fit between printing and design, he refinanced his home to raise the capital he needed to obtain a lease and the necessary equipment. He borrowed from other sources, as well, which left him heavily in debt to his family and friends.

Harry secured an expensive lease in a growth area of a large metropolitan area. The location was very desirable, and he believed it would bring in a lot of the foot traffic that is critical for a quick printer. As Harry's idea unfolded, the concept of a quick printer became overshadowed as he planned to do more sophisticated print work than quick printing.

More extensive printing requires more equipment. So, armed with all of his remaining capital, Harry bought as much printing equipment as he could—not clear about how he would use it or how he could provide for a return on his investment. He bought presses, copiers, a fax machine, a paper cutter, and much more.

Opening day came. The equipment was hardly used; not much more than an occasional copy was made. As the weeks passed, the quick printing equipment got the most use. The other, more sophisticated printing equipment remained dormant.

As the months passed, it became clear that much of Harry's capital had been invested in equipment that did not get used and, therefore, brought no return on his investment. Since he had used all of his capital for equipment, Harry did not have any money to spend on advertising; he had no time to market the business, because he had to work the counter to attend to his walk-in customers. And, he did not have a way to sell the more sophisticated two-color printing capability, so the equipment sat unused.

Slowly, the quick printing business began to prosper because of Harry's endurance and willingness to work long hours. He made enough money to pay the rent and his basic bills, but was not able to accrue any excess to promote the more lucrative printing business. The fancy machines sat, collecting dust.

Analysis

Where did Harry go wrong?

Why didn't Harry realize his dream of owning a successful printing and graphic design business?

What role did equipment play in his mistake?

Harry's mistake was classic. He thought he had to have all the equipment to open his doors to do business. He did not realize what it would take to run a quick printing business and graphic design studio, and a two-color printing business.

He did not take into account the substantial labor required to grow a quick printing business that dictates that the retail counter be manned all the time. He also did not realize the resources needed to launch a two-color printing business. Sources of this business are referrals from graphic designers, direct contact with prospects, and advertising, rather than foot traffic. Harry did not have the money to advertise; he had no time to call on prospects because he was needed at the retail store counter and to do the quick printing.

Harry should not have purchased the fancy printing equipment. He should have used the capital to promote aggressively the quick printing business. Once the quick printing was producing the income he was expecting, he would have been in a position to purchase specialized printing equipment.

Many start-up business owners overbuy. Perhaps it makes them feel they are serious about going into business—that they have made a commitment. This is not good business and it leads to a sense of false security; the business looks like it is established when, in reality, it is not. Many start-up businesses mistakenly want to emulate those that are already successfully established. They think they must have all the equipment from the beginning. This wipes out their scarce resources.

Business owners need to understand that businesses make money when they understand how to generate sales for the various types of equipment. By itself, equipment does not make money.

Lessons to Be Learned

Prove to yourself that you will almost immediately use the items you invest in. If you tie up your scarce resources in equipment that you do not use, you will not get the return on investment that you must have to be successful.

Your investment in marketing is a capital investment with an expected return. Typically, start-up businesses do not expend enough capital to get the business going successfully. Even more importantly, the capital that they invest is often not invested wisely. Most is spent on equipment—the trappings of being an established business— and not enough is spent on activities that make money— marketing and promotion.

► List the equipment you *need* to have to start your business.

► What return on investment do you expect in the next six months?

► Does your marketing plan include specific goals and a budget to achieve those goals?

See also *Marketing Your Consulting or Professional Services*, by David Karlson, Ph.D., Crisp Publications; *Starting Your New Business: A Guide for Entrepreneurs*, by Charles L. Martin, Ph.D., Crisp Publications; *Understanding Financial Statements*, by James O. Gill, Crisp Publications.

CASE STUDY

Uncontrolled Growth—Small Is Beautiful!

Many first-time business owners go by only what they know. This is limiting when it comes to handling money and choosing a growth strategy.

In this case study, Dennis and his partner lost their once highly successful business because they did not have a realistic growth strategy.

Dennis was exceptionally well trained as a mechanic for foreign cars. Considered very talented by people in the foreign car repair business, he even knew how to repair foreign car transmissions—a rare skill in the foreign car repair community. And, he became particularly skilled on one upscale manufacturer's models, which was lucrative to repair. Dennis was clearly not a rank-and-file mechanic.

For several years, Dennis had worked for auto repair shops in the Washington, DC, area, one of the major foreign car markets in the United States. He dreamed of finding gold on the West Coast. When he was approached by another mechanic with a similar background and capability who had a dream like Dennis's, he set out with his new friend to earn fame and fortune in California.

The two set up a shop in Los Angeles, which had an even larger market for foreign cars than Washington, DC. They had enough savings to open a small, upscale foreign car repair facility in a good location. Their market research paid off, as well as their modest promotion efforts that were targeted at a very active manufacturer's make auto club. Club members quickly spread the word about their new garage, where the owners knew how to treat customers well, did reliable work, and charged fair prices.

During the next four years, their small garage that rented for $1,000 per month with two mechanics experienced phenomenal growth. The story of their success looked like an experience everyone would want to emulate. They put all their excess capital back into the business; since their overhead was low, this was substantial. The more they made, the more they spent on equipment. For example, they purchased several new lifts that cost $10,000 each.

After the first year, they moved into a more upscale facility that rented for $6,000 per month. The new facility opened new growth opportunities, since they had space to employ more mechanics to deal with the ever-increasing demand for their services.

In the second year, they hired four very competent mechanics who performed the type of top service that their customers were accustomed too. These mechanics increased overhead substantially; they each needed a lift and tools, and each averaged a yearly salary of $65,000. Yet, demand for their services continued to be strong, and word had spread fast in the foreign car community that this was a quality shop, well worth the premium cost for repairs.

During the third year, Dennis and his partner opened an auto body shop. They rented even more space and bought specialized equipment to do auto body work, with state-of-the-art painting capability. They hired the best auto body repair staff around, which again increased their overhead. Their goal was to make wrecked cars look like they came out of the factory, and Dennis and his partner accomplished that. Word spread fast and the new venture was a success.

At the four-year mark they employed a staff of twenty-two people and were just able to meet their monthly overhead. Having purchased the equipment on time, their debt was very high. They continued to put any excess funds back into the business. Since they were at capacity, they could not take on any new customers. They geared up to serve their customers and to add staff.

The recession that hit the country during their fifth year was devastating to California. Business slowed down considerably as the recession hit the upper-middle class. Many of their customers lost their jobs, since the aerospace industry was one of the hardest hit. Revenues slackened by 25 percent and the partners were unable to pay some bills.

The business was too far leveraged; they could not withstand a downturn in the economy. Each month they came closer to financial ruin. They could not pay the rent or the loans for all the equipment they had purchased. Finally, their business collapsed and they had to declare Chapter 11.

Analysis

Where did Dennis and his partner go wrong?

What business decisions got Dennis and his partner into trouble?

What could Dennis and his partner have done to stabilize their business?

When Dennis and his partner started their business they knew nothing about the business side of their venture. They knew what customers wanted and they knew what they could deliver. And deliver they did.

They grew the business too fast. They racked up too much debt. They did not set up a reserve fund to withstand a slow period; their cash flow was all they could call upon to pay their bills. Since they were so far extended, when the cash flow began to dry up, they were immediately in trouble—in debt and saddled with a very high monthly overhead.

Their method of growing the business had worked for four years. They reinvested everything they made. Since they never took out any of the profits, after four years they were right where they were when they started.

The partners had not improved their personal financial positions either. They followed the model that they knew— grow the business by putting everything back into it. It worked for four years. Then the bottom fell out.

Dennis and his partner could have stabilized their business by growing it more slowly. They could have done this by *not* putting everything back into it, by saving some for emergencies, and by taking some profits for themselves. They ran up debts too fast for equipment and rental. They added staff to meet the demand when they should have let the demand exceed the supply.

Lessons to Be Learned

Initial success fooled Dennis and his partner into thinking that their fortune would continue forever. They never anticipated the rapid change brought about by the economy, so they were not prepared to deal with it.

When you choose a strategy to grow your business, be aware of all the possibilities that can have a powerful impact on your business. Many of these—such as a change in the political climate—are completely out of your control.

Success is wonderful. Yet, it can be deceiving and devastating if you do not handle it carefully. To chart the waters of success, make sure you have a solid understanding of the basics of financial management.

Your Turn   ***Answer the following questions:***

► Do you have a plan for the financial growth of your business?

► List potential outside forces that could influence your business.

See also *Understanding Financial Statements*, by James O. Gill, Crisp Publications; *Financial Basics of Small Business Success*, by James O. Gill, Crisp Publications.

ASK YOURSELF

► Explain how you will make money in the business you are considering.

► Describe your plans for financial management.

► Discuss your plans for expansion.

► How realistically have you projected your expenditures and income?

CHAPTER SIX

BUSINESS RELATIONSHIP MISTAKES

COSTS OF CONFLICT

Conflict and disagreement are fundamental to business life. Indeed, diverse opinions and conflicting ideas are traditional ingredients in any creative, productive enterprise. Business owners would like to believe that all of the conflicts within a business can be resolved smoothly. But many are poorly equipped to sort through what is fact and what is feeling in a dispute with another business partner.

Left unattended, simmering conflicts in a business can be costly. Conflict among the principals of a business creates ripples of strain that are felt throughout the business. Trust goes out the window, morale slides, and even customers can sense that something is wrong. Some disputes may go unresolved, festering for months or even years, until they erupt with disastrous consequences.

Conflict occurs in each of the three basic stages of the business cycle:

1. *Formation and start-up stage*
   In the first stage, issues of purpose, direction and business intent are shaped by the way principals perceive and understand their relationships with one another.

2. *Operational stage*
   In the second stage, potential conflicts may emerge over how best to run the business and how to manage relationships between owners in a smooth and functional manner.

3. *Transitional stage*
   In the third stage, acquisitions, mergers, sale, succession, dissolution or change in top leadership may occur. New relationships need to be managed and old relationships need to be settled.

Workplace relationships often involve a tangle of business and interpersonal issues. People who join and work with one another in a business enterprise are brought together by past social or professional association. They are drawn together by the common business objectives they share.

As the case studies in this chapter illustrate, mistakes made in managing relationships and resolving conflicts with business partners at any stage in the business cycle can spell the difference between success and failure of a business.

CASE STUDY

A Partnership of Unequals

An independent working relationship with a business colleague is not the same as a working relationship with a supervisor or fellow employee within a company framework.

As Ben and Ron found out the hard way in this case study, if you set up a formal agreement at start-up, you can avoid a lot of misunderstandings, and increase your chances of maintaining a smooth working relationship.

Ben and Ron worked together in a consulting practice that gives advice on securing patents for companies with newly developed products. The firm helps companies sell the rights for their inventions and new products in both domestic and overseas markets. They add value by matching up producers of new products with distributors and wholesalers in the supply chain. Their work consists of customer and market analysis, product evaluation, and feasibility studies of new technology potential.

Ben started the consulting practice after twenty-five years as a technology transfer specialist in a major computer hardware company. He has traveled widely, lectures at a prestigious university, and has the respect of many industry experts and innovators.

Ron was fresh out of an MBA program. He came to the firm with about a year of consulting experience, a high-technology background and a lot of professional energy to burn.

The relationship between Ben and Ron began when Ben landed several consulting projects and saw that he would be swamped by the workload. Ron had been a student in one of the graduate school courses Ben had taught. Ben thought highly of Ron's academic work and thought process.

Ben contacted Ron to ask if he could "help him out." Ron had done some independent consulting throughout his MBA program and was no stranger to the perils and opportunities of consulting. When Ben's request came along, it was too good for Ron to turn down.

Midway through the second feasibility study, Ron realized how much he knew about inventions, new product development and technology transfer. The unique combination of skills he learned in business school, coupled with the scientific knowledge he had accumulated by consulting with technology firms while he was in school, had made him a real asset for this kind of work.

While it felt good to be working right out of school, Ron wondered about the relationship he had with Ben. Was it one where he was the apprentice and Ben was the mentor? Was he the employee and Ben the employer? Were they equals in this consulting business? Or, were they two guys who had gotten together to take advantage of a consulting opportunity?

These questions came to Ron as he contemplated the difference between their billing rates. Ben billed his time at $90 an hour; Ron's time was billed at $40 an hour. Their net income was about half of their billing rates. The balance covered overhead of the business, which was Ben's.

As time passed and more consulting work rolled in, Ron realized how much of a role he played in generating new business. He was responsible for landing three of the last four contracts. While these contracts were small compared to the one that Ben brought in, they indicated that he had potential for getting more of this kind of work.

From Ron's point of view it seemed that this was the time to discuss a more fair billing arrangement with Ben. He talked to some of his professional colleagues about the rates they were billing and began to document what he thought he was worth in the marketplace.

Ron's rationale for getting a higher net salary for the work he was doing with Ben went something like this:

- ► He was currently getting only about two-thirds of the salary level that his fellow MBA colleagues were getting.

- ► He was not getting any health insurance, vacation or retirement benefits.

- ► Ben's overhead expenses were minimal, since the business was being run out of Ben's home and they used temporary and part-time support staff.

- ► Ron had done consulting work while he was in graduate school, and had earned rates equal to and higher than he was getting now.

Ron believed he was "loaded for bear" and set up a meeting to discuss his billing rates and his future relationship with Ben.

At the meeting, Ben listened to Ron's arguments. He responded by saying that he was concerned about having Ron in any kind of an employee relationship, since he did not want to be burdened by filing withholding and unemployment taxes for anyone.

Ron felt that Ben was being esoteric, avoiding the issue, and needlessly worried about the IRS. Ron stated that he wanted to be paid for the value he brought to this enterprise. Ben retorted that he could have Dick, one of his old work colleagues who had retired, handle the work that Ron was doing in half the time it took Ron to complete the job. Ron responded "you wouldn't have even the necessary money to cover your overhead if it weren't for me."

They fumed at each other for another hour before stalking out of the meeting without a clue as to where they stood with one another. After a few days, Ron called Ben and asked to meet to continue the discussion. Ben said he felt that a trust between the two had been broken. He was wary of another shouting match with Ron, but was willing to talk.

At their next meeting, Ben spoke more calmly and stated how differently he saw the billing rates than Ron. Ron choked up, feeling he had reached a dead-end in his attempt to break into this type of business.

They had come to an impasse, and were unable to agree on even the basic element of compensation. All the hard-earned business that Ron had brought in did not seem to matter to Ben. Ron felt exploited and dejected. He wondered what he was going to do at this point—work for apprentice-level wages after having helped build the business?

Ron left the meeting not knowing where to turn. He did not believe that going back to work with Ben at $40 an hour would do anything to save him face professionally. He knew now that he had some consulting potential in this future, and that he also needed experience with a mentor. Unfortunately, Ben did not show Ron a willingness to provide that at a satisfactory salary level.

After a week of brooding, Ron contacted Ben to see about the status of several proposals that were to be awarded. He was shocked to learn that Ben had brought in Dick to handle the consulting duties that Ron had handled over the past 18 months. Ron was angry. He thought about filing a lawsuit against Ben and the business, but was advised by an attorney friend of his that "he didn't have a leg to stand on."

Sadly, Ron decided to move to another state to reconstruct his professional career.

Analysis

What went wrong?

What mistake did Ron make?

Ron failed to identify from the start what he wanted for himself in the consulting relationship. Therefore, he was not in a position to identify his interests in any formal agreement with Ben. Ron failed to set up terms agreement that provided for his income needs and met his career development expectations.

In business, it is crucial to identify your needs and interests, to articulate them in draft agreement language, and then to negotiate the best arrangement possible. Without clarity on Ron's part, he became a victim of an undefined partnership.

Lessons to Be Learned

When two independent business entities (as Ron and Ben were) join forces, that relationship can range from very casual, to informal with a handshake, to a formal written agreement. Ron failed to see himself as a business entity.

By treating the relationship with Ben as an implicit employer/ employee agreement, he set up a hierarchy that put Ben on top and him on the bottom.

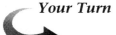

Your Turn

Answer the following questions:

- ► Are you clear about what your professional interests, career path, and income needs are?

- ► Are you able to draft the initial version of the kind of agreement you want?

- ► From whom can you seek advice about the points in your agreement?

- ► Do you know the process or manner in which you want your agreement to be negotiated?

See also *Can This Partnership Be Saved? Improving (or Salvaging) Your Key Business Relationships* by Peter Wylie and Mardy Grothe, Upstart Publishing, 1993.

CASE STUDY

Too Many Players on the Field

In a collaborative venture, each person's motives and commitment can have a major impact on the success of the venture. Be sure these are articulated and agreed upon, or you may find yourself failing to balance the business interests of your team.

The venture in this case study disintegrated because the team failed to articulate and agree on their motives and commitment.

The setting was a chic, after-theater party in a mansion on the fashionable side of town, complemented by an attractive array of native crafts and art work from Central America. The blend of modern and traditional artwork and crafts had the crowd oohing and ahhing. Many of the guests remarked how charming it was and how all these crafts fit so well with the architecture of the mansion.

Clustered in one corner of the dining room, three women talked about how the crowd responded with such interest and receptiveness to the native crafts and artwork that was positioned throughout the mansion. If this crowd responded so positively to these pieces of art, would others be as interested?

As they talked further, a business scheme began to unfold. Could they go to the various Central American countries, find the craftsmen and artists—and others like them—who produced these works, and bring them into urban areas of the United States where buyers with sophisticated tastes would eagerly purchase the artifacts at what would certainly turn out to be attractive prices? This seemed like a natural entrepreneurial opportunity.

The would-be players in this entrepreneurial game were Deena, Kathy and Maria. All friends, they had common interests in native art; each woman was searching to match her interests in arts and crafts with some form of economic livelihood.

Deena had an international consulting background and had worked and traveled in Latin America. She had connections with the wife of a Latin American ambassador, and was interested in finding a way to blend work and pleasure. On the verge of becoming burned out with the consulting regimen, she was looking for another way to make money and grow a new business.

Kathy was a former marketing agent for a clothing manufacturer. She currently managed a household. Her connection to Latin America was through the manufacturer she had represented, which had its production facility in Latin America. During her tenure with the company, she had visited the facility several times and had come back with armloads of artwork and native crafts that now decorated her house. She was looking for a way to make extra money, although she was not interested in risking too much, since she was raising two small children.

A native of Costa Rica, Maria was employed by a bank that provided financing for many Latin American development projects. She traveled widely throughout Latin America as part of her banking business and had an understanding of craft businesses as micro-enterprises in Latin America. She was an avid collector of Latin American art.

Each of the women knew others who had similar interests and dreams of growing a business; these other associates became "silent partners" and quite soon it seemed that this venture was ready to take off.

All of the women had stated that they were friends at the start, and that they wanted to remain friends throughout this venture. But as they began to sort through who was going to do what, who would be paid how much, and when they would get a return on their investment, the conflicts began to arise between them.

Deena proposed that she combine a buying trip in Costa Rica with some consulting on an analysis of economic conditions she had just landed there. Rather innocently, this first set of business choices turned into a squabble. For example, Kathy wondered if Deena would be focused simply on items that she liked, or be able to find crafts that would realistically be sellable. Maria worried whether Deena had a sense of design that would enable her to make selections of crafts that would sell. Maria became upset that the connections she had cultivated in Latin America would be bypassed and leave her feeling unneeded as a team member.

The silent partners in the venture were not so sure that this was the best way to buy the first installment of crafts. What would happen if the selections that Deena made turned out to be "duds"? How would the venture recover from having made a bad impression in the arts and crafts marketplace?

The "active" players began to see the "passive" investors as meddlesome. Agreement over who had responsibility for the primary tasks of marketing, selling and distribution became clouded as the members of the venture team struggled to sort out what was the best way to satisfy both the active and the passive investors. After several months of "gridlock" and missed buying opportunities, the lucrative Christmas season was upon them; they had no products to offer the outlets to whom they had, by this time, made promises.

Over time, the "friends" who started the venture ended up not speaking to one another and feeling alienated. Several of the passive investors soured on the business idea. All the players in this venture came out as losers, both financially and interpersonally.

Analysis

What went wrong?

What mistake did these players make?

The members of this venture team failed to be candid with each other about their personal and business motives. They forged ahead without a clear understanding of how each investor would fit into the total picture. They did not recognize the need for two types of strategy and business structure:

one for a start-up period and another, more formal one, for an operational phase of the venture.

Lessons to Be Learned

In a collective team effort such as this one, it is very important to have a written agreement, or at least a common understanding of what each person's contribution to the venture will be. It is easy to get caught up in the romance of a business idea and forget that each person may have unique motives guiding his or her involvement. Likewise, each person may have a different level of commitment, as evidenced by the desire to be either an active or passive investor.

Your Turn

Answer the following questions:

► Do all members on your team have roles?

► List your motives for being in this business venture.

1.

2.

3.

4.

5.

6.

► Do you understand the motives of your venture partners?

► Do you have an agreement for the type of business structure you will use in your venture?

See also *Collaborating: Finding Common Ground For Multiparty Problems*, by Barbara Gray, Jossey-Bass Publishers, 1989.

CASE STUDY

What Business Are We In Anyway?

A basic mistake that business partners who were former professional colleagues make is believing that their current business relationship will be like the one they had in the past. Therefore, they often do not clarify the relationship and the mission of their start-up business.

Bill and Mack learned the painful lesson of this case study when their business venture collapsed in less than one year.

In the four years that Bill and Mack had worked together at the Department of Defense, they established a rapport that was personally and professionally comfortable. They left to pursue separate professional paths in the private sector at about the same time—Bill as an entrepreneur and Mack as a project manager in a large engineering firm.

Years later, after keeping in contact at conferences and visits to each other's offices, they decided to team up again and build upon Bill's established business base. Mack would provide the hard-driving management skills needed to get projects done on time and keep clients happy. Bill would be freed up to bring in new business and manage the company overall.

It seemed like old times. Bill and Mack were together again, taking on some of the same challenges they had as a team in the past, while looking for new business in a market that seemed ripe for their combined skills and experience.

One difference was evident, however. In his continuous pursuit of new ideas and new business, Bill had developed a very high-technology orientation. He knew all the "cutting edge" computer programs and their potential applications in the field. On the other hand, Mack was a novice with personal computers. He still did things the old-fashioned way, with sharp drafting pencils and graph paper. These tools had served him well in the large firm he was with over the years.

The differences in their styles became differences in their approach to the work, differences in staff allegiance within the company, and ultimately, differences in the kinds of new work that Bill and Mack each sought for the company.

From the beginning of their new venture, Bill sensed that he and Mack had conflicting business goals. Bill saw the company moving to apply "cutting edge" technologies that could be used in non-traditional ways for new customers. Mack saw the company as more traditional, serving traditional clients in traditional, nontechnical ways.

After six months of conflict about where the business was headed, the initial marketing effort sputtered and staff morale plummeted. Employees were confused about whose ideas were the source of leadership in the company. Finally, Bill and Mack decided that they needed to do some strategic planning and get some advice about the direction to point their company.

They did what many small companies do: they hired a consultant to prepare a business plan and marketing strategy, and looked forward to getting their working relationship and their business focus back on track again.

Believing that he had no option but to move ahead and be in control, Bill took matters into his own hands and worked directly with the strategic planning consultant to craft a mission statement for the company. They put together a statement that reflected Bill's ideas exclusively, expressed in language that sounded foreign to Mack.

Mack did not understand how Bill could put a mission statement together for the company without his input. Wasn't he a major player in the company? Mack had thought he was, but now he was not sure. Was Bill trying to take the business down a path of uncertainty and risk?

Fearing the worst, Mack began meeting secretly with other staff members with whom he shared his concerns about where the business was headed. The office staff soon divided into separate camps with separate allegiances. Cooperation between project teams broke down, and Mack began to enlist staff members to leave the company and start up a new venture with him at its head.

Bill had observed Mack's activities, and had tolerated them without trying to understand why Mack was doing what he was doing. As Mack became more and more critical of the direction the business was going, Bill became more and more alienated. With Mack considering leaving the company and taking some key staff members with him, it looked as though Bill might have a full-scale staff revolt on his hands.

Analysis

What went wrong?

Where did Bill and Mack make their mistakes?

Mack believed that he could treat Bill in the same subordinate manner that he had in their past business relationship. However, the tables were turned: This was Bill's business and Bill was going to steer it in the direction he wanted. Bill was not even clear about why he wanted Mack to join the business and what he expected from him.

When Mack got a vague message from Bill about what Bill expected, he made an assumption that Bill would be willing to operate in the same manner the two of them had operated before.

While Mack was naive in assuming that his past relationship with Bill was enough of a basis to establish trust and understanding between them, Bill failed to lay out the terms of their new relationship. To Mack, they seemed to be equal partners professionally, if not financially. To Bill, the relationship was clearly one where his business was now in need of some of the skills Mack so ably demonstrated in their past working relationship.

While Bill was in charge now, he was reluctant to confront Mack with the reality that Bill's ideas would be the direction the company would go. This reluctance, along with their vague relationship, made it difficult for them to work together effectively.

Lessons to Be Learned

There are many ways to establish and clarify relationships with business partners. If you fail to do so at the initial stages of the relationship, you will miss the best opportunity to do so.

Holding on to a past impression of someone's competence in a fast-changing business climate can lead to strained relationships and costly down-time for a new business. Be certain about the motives people have for teaming up with you in your business. Ask them what their business goals are. If they do not expect to push in the same direction, they may not belong on your team.

Your Turn   *Answer the following questions:*

► Are you clear about the type of business you are in and the kind of team you need?

► Can you recognize what type of business talent best suits your company's needs?

See also *Getting Together: Building a Relationship That Gets To YES*, by Roger Fisher and Scott Brown, Houghton Mifflin Company, 1988.

CASE STUDY

What You See is What You Get

As Tim and Don learned in this case study, failing to agree on how to manage your relationship with a business vendor can be costly in financial terms as well as in trust.

Tim and Don got together for a drink at the opening-night reception of a national conference for software engineers. The preconference workshop on marketing they had just attended together revealed a strong similarity in their business interests. They discovered that they had a mutual interest in developing a software program to assist publishers in putting textbooks onto floppy disks for easy reference and learning of technical material.

They committed to following up with additional meetings to verify their common interests and their desire to collaborate. Once they returned to their respective offices in the same metropolitan area, they began the venture development process in earnest.

One of the first items of business was to develop a brochure that would communicate the value of their tool to potential clients in the publishing industry. While they both saw the need for the brochure, they acknowledged that they did not have a clear statement of their business mission. Nevertheless, they felt they needed to act quickly; the window of opportunity for this idea might close down on them rather quickly. They agreed to forge ahead and seek out a graphic design and public relations firm to help produce the marketing vehicle they needed.

Through their past work in the area, they each knew several firms that did this kind of work. They decided to create a competition among several candidate firms to see what they had to offer, and select the one whose approach suited them best. After meeting with several firms they had each worked with previously, they offered them a trial assignment:

develop a sketch plan for the brochure with some initial text to communicate the idea.

When the preliminary sketches were presented, one clearly stood out as special and unique in its approach and appeal. The two business partners quickly agreed on which graphics and public relations firm would produce the brochure.

Executing the contract for this service was another matter. Don had little experience in dealing with business-to-business service vendors. Working with the public relations firm was new for him. Accustomed to overseeing carefully the details of work done by his staff, he used written edits and feedback in notes on draft materials to manage the vendor. Don felt it was important to articulate the details of the language that the public relations firm would use in the brochure copy.

Tim tended to rely on the expertise of the public relations firm and react to what creativity it had to offer in its proposed drafts of copy material.

Gradually, the working relationship between Don and Tim as clients and the public relations firm as the vendor began to deteriorate. Don was unhappy with the way the vendor was performing. His edits were not readily accepted, and he always seemed to be faced with a line of reasoning from the vendor he did not want to hear.

On the other hand, Tim was trying to maintain a cooperative working relationship with the vendor, to encourage the most creative effort.

Often, the vendor would complain to Tim about Don's "off-base view" of what this business opportunity really was. As a public relations expert, the vendor believed he knew how to communicate a message that would really reach their potential customers.

As the draft of the brochure went through repeated revisions, the public relations firm avoided Don and "shopped for approval" with Tim, since he had the "friendly ear." Don began to feel alienated and resented that he was left out of what he believed were important decisions about the new business.

Taking advantage of what was now emerging as a split in the unity about the brochure text, the vendor played Tim and Don off against one another. They could send draft materials to Tim and Don in sequential fashion, with the implication that one partner had already approved the version that the other partner was being asked to review.

As more and more drafts of the text were required to satisfy Don's sense of quality and image about the business, Tim's frustration with the process began to show. He was ready to accept almost anything to get through the process. The vendor was becoming increasingly frustrated with the lack of closure and acceptance after offering so many drafts. Finally, the vendor simply "fired the client," and refused to do any more work on the brochure.

The result was not an obvious disaster, but Tim and Don were left with a half-baked version of the brochure that they had really needed to get their business off the ground.

What really damaged their relationship was the loss of mutual confidence and energy that the two had started their venture with, and the lost opportunity to use the development of their brochure to articulate what their business mission was all about.

Analysis

What went wrong?

Where did Tim and Don make their mistake?

One stumbling block for Tim and Don was their reluctance to discuss and allocate responsibility for managing their relationship with this business vendor. The lack of clarity between them as clients produced an ambiguous response from the vendor.

They also failed to sit down and develop a company mission statement before they engaged outside business services. Without clarity between them on their business purpose, they were not likely to give clear direction to a marketing vendor who was trying to assist them.

Lessons to Be Learned

Be certain that all team members of the venture are satisfied and committed to retaining the business vendors who are helping you build your business. Do not hesitate to "air your dirty laundry" in-house. Reluctance to face potential conflicts over vendor support and performance can be costly in both financial terms as well as trust. Avoid three-way relationships—"triangles." These tend to produce faulty perception and communication.

Your Turn

Answer the following questions:

▶ Write a paragraph that describes the purpose of and expectations for the business vendor you want to hire.

▶ Does your contract with a business vendor make clear who has review, approval and payment responsibility?

▶ What in-house ground rules do you have for working with outside business vendors?

See also *Collaborating: Finding Common Ground For Multiparty Problems*, by Barbara Gray, Jossey-Bass Publishers, 1989.

CASE STUDY

Who Decides Who Decides?

As Sam and Myron found out in this case study, not having ground rules for making day-to-day decisions with a business partner can lead to major disputes.

Sam and Myron had worked together for six years as employees of a family-owned publishing business with a reputation for high-quality, creative work, That reputation was largely a result of Sam's and Myron's efforts. However, as nonfamily employees they knew that their future growth opportunities in this company were limited.

When the company founder passed away, the other family employees decided to discontinue the business. The family agreed to sell the company name and the goodwill that came with it to Sam and Myron, and the two former employees found themselves in business together as owners.

The two new business partners had worked well together as a team, under the supervision of the publishing company's founder. He was a crusty veteran of the business world, who knew instinctively how to recognize a problem and to solve it. Regrettably, he was not much of a mentor. Neither Sam and Myron nor any of the family employees were tutored by the company's founder before he died. That left much for these two new business partners to learn.

Sam's business style was very entrepreneurial and "big picture." He had been raised in a fairly wealthy family; much of his early years had been planned out for him, and he breezed through college with a liberal arts degree. Never really having to work for a living, he discovered that he liked "chasing new business" and the satisfaction that came with landing a new account.

In contrast, Myron was an immigrant whose family was well-off by the standards of his native country, but who came to the United States with little more than the shirt on his back. He received a traditional education and learned the skills of a graphic designer. To be able to hold down an important, responsible job was a source of pride to both Myron and his family, who still lived in his native land and to whom he occasionally sent money orders to upgrade their standard of living.

It took some time for the two partners to get their business going. After a year or so, they were generating enough revenue from former customers of the old family-owned company to pay their bills and to scrape by. Each partner felt equally responsible for landing the business and for bringing in customers of the family-owned company. Things seemed to be progressing well from an external perspective.

However, from the inside all was not well. Tensions were growing over the way each partner made—and did not make—a range of decisions.

The business hours the two put in were substantially different, which led to a laissez-faire approach around how the two of them used their time in the business. Sam tended to do what was needed to get new business, and "spent 24 hours a day" thinking about the business and opportunities for it. On the other hand, Myron saw his workday much the same as he did when he was an employee. He came in at 8 A.M. and worked steadily until 5 P.M. When he left for the day, his time was his own. While he often thought about the business, he did not conduct any business when he was out of the office.

Making business decisions in other areas was also ambiguous. It was not clear when would be the best time for them to hire additional employees for the new work they were bringing in. Given the many trade-offs to be considered, choices around where they would locate their new offices were difficult. Even deciding on how office supply purchases would be made and who would make them presented the two partners with challenges that only seemed to produce tension, not results.

While the tensions grew about how decisions ought to be made, the pace of new customers began to drop off. Myron began to discount Sam's value for bringing in new business. Myron became more aloof and stressed, believing that he was holding the business together with his steady day-to-day commitment to producing the work. Sam began to consider that things were not working out as smoothly as he planned, and started to look for a third partner for the business.

For several months, Myron and Sam tried to sort through how they would make their business decisions—from the basic to the most important ones. Most of these efforts ended in shouting matches, with one or the other partner walking out of the meeting.

It was not long before they were conferring with their attorneys and looking for a way to break up the partnership. The partnership dispute ended up as a court battle, which is not uncommon when partners cannot figure out a way to work together.

Analysis

What went wrong?

Where did Sam and Myron go wrong?

Sam and Myron had little understanding of their business as a system of decisions and the extent of variance in their decision-making styles. Without a sense of implicit trust between the partners, they had to construct an approach to use when deciding business issues. They were unable to do this, and they failed to recognize that they needed to.

Lessons to Be Learned

Business partners cannot always rely on trust between each other. It may not always be there, even when partners have the will to work together. Motivation to have the business be successful is, by itself, not sufficient either.

Answer the following questions:

► List the basic types of decisions you need to make in your business.

1.

2.

3.

4.

5.

► Is your decision-making style different than that of your business partner's? If so, how is it different?

► When will a decision in your business be joint? Individual? Deferential? By consensus?

See also *Getting To YES: Negotiating Agreement Without Giving In*, by Roger Fisher and William Ury, Penguin Books, 1983.

CASE STUDY

Power Behind The Throne

In this case study, Dawn learned two painful lessons when she set up an agreement that did not anticipate the realities of her assignment and did not consider the influence of personal and family relationships in the agreement.

In the second year of her new business of planning and managing meetings and conferences for companies and associations, Dawn was well on her way to being an established success. She had a strong base of West Coast clients from contacts she had made at her previous job as director of public relations for a major software manufacturer in California's Silicon Valley.

Dawn was aware that she would need to market beyond California to grow her business significantly, so she followed the calendar of conferences and events sponsored by East Coast-based organizations that were holding events in the San Francisco area. Visiting these events provided a great networking opportunity for her.

At the annual conference of a software engineering association that was based on the east coast, Dawn met with Judy, the association's executive director. The conference program was well designed and interesting, but the attendance levels were so low that it was evident to Dawn that they were going to lose money on the event.

Dawn mentioned this to Judy, and suggested several improvements in the way the conference might be marketed in the future. Judy concurred with her analysis and was impressed with Dawn's assessment. Judy suggested they talk after the conference about the possibility of working together to make the next year's event a better one.

Several months after the conference, the financial results turned out to be worse than anyone had expected. Martin, the association's founder, asked Judy to initiate a discussion with Dawn to retain her for meeting planning and marketing services. Martin's wife, Penny, also on the association's board of directors, agreed that an external planner who could handle on-site arrangements would improve the chances of success of the next year's conference.

Dawn proposed terms for the agreement: she would handle all site selection, facility arrangements and space rental for vendor displays. The association would be responsible for program design, marketing and registration. Given the geographic separation of the association from her office and the conference location for the next year, this seemed to be a reasonable division of labor.

Dawn's fee for services was based on fixed costs plus a percentage of the registration revenue at the conference. It was not a complicated formula for Dawn, who had used it before. While Judy was familiar with the formula, she had a difficult time convincing Martin and Penny that Judy's fee structure was standard in the conference-planning business.

Because of the delay caused by "due diligence" considerations by Penny, the planning time for the conference had lapsed; they were on the verge of being too late for an effective marketing effort. Dawn urged the association to take action quickly and to approve a contract with her.

Fearing that they would face a disaster if they did not act promptly, and anticipating that the contract would be formally approved shortly, Judy and Dawn informally agreed to have Dawn proceed with preparations. On this informal basis, Dawn began her work to assist the association in planning its next conference.

Several months before the conference was scheduled to occur, the contract was signed by Penny and Judy faxed it to Dawn. Now the pressure was on to meet marketing, publicity and registration goals sufficiently in advance of the conference, to ensure it would be successful. Everyone became acutely aware of the reality of deadlines that would be extremely difficult to meet.

As might be expected, the short timetable led to less-than-effective marketing and publicity for the conference; attendance was poor. When it was time to allocate fees and costs for the conference, a squabble occurred. Dawn had a signed contract, but Penny asserted that Dawn had not done the promotional job on-site that she had promised; Penny claimed that attendance had been low because of Dawn's poor promotion.

Judy acknowledged that Dawn's performance was acceptable under the difficult conditions she had to work with, but she needed Martin and Penny's approval to pay Dawn. And, the association had not yet done an accounting of costs for the conference to determine its net income and Dawn's fee.

At this point in the process, Penny asked the association's attorneys to look into the obligations and liabilities they had to Dawn. Martin left the decision-making to Judy and Penny.

More than a year after the conference, Dawn has not been paid for her work. She has threatened to file a lawsuit against the association, which has still not provided a final cost accounting of the conference. Judy has moved on to another job at another association. Penny says she wants to settle the matter by negotiating an agreement, but Dawn says that she had a valid agreement with Judy, and she will accept nothing less than the fee that was proposed in their initial agreement.

Analysis

What went wrong?

Where did Dawn make her mistake?

Dawn failed to propose an agreement flexible enough to accommodate conditions that could not be predicted with mathematical accuracy. With her conference-planning experience, she should have been able to anticipate that the planning cycle for this conference was too short to be completed under a standard contract format, where time and trust are on the side of both parties.

Lessons to Be Learned

When you negotiate an agreement with an organization that has more than one "talking head," be sure you know who is in charge. In retrospect, it was clear that Penny was calling the shots.

The negotiation process is an integral part of the process of reaching an agreement, for the level of a fee, for the scope of work and for the timetable for performance. Make sure the negotiation process is a deliberate step by both parties to reach an agreement that is satisfactory for both.

Answer the following questions:

- ▶ Do you know all of the people involved in your contract agreements?

- ▶ Do you know the power relationships between parties with whom you are negotiating agreements?

- ▶ Does your negotiation include a fail-safe way for you to get paid?

See also *Deal Maker: All The Negotiating Skills And Secrets You Need*, by Robert Lawrence Kuhn, John Wiley & Sons, 1988.

CASE STUDY

Your Turn To Pick Up The Check

Misunderstandings about how business expenses will be shared with your business partner(s) can result in distrust and, as Bob, Jack and Barry found out in this case study, dissolution of the partnership.

Bob, Jack and Barry began their business relationship after they met in an MBA program. Each of the three budding entrepreneurs excelled in his coursework. They recognized a common zeal for starting a new business that stood out from others in their class. Their business plan projects were so high quality that they had all been approached by local venture capitalists seeking to invest in their start-up businesses.

Recognizing their common interests and that none of them was ready to jump into a formal business relationship with an investor who might want to dictate how they would pursue their business ideas, they decided to combine forces for mutual support.

This loose relationship was more for incubation support than it was for strategic business purposes. While the three had business ideas that related to computer applications in an office environment, they each sought a slightly different niche in the marketplace.

Bob was developing a series of programs to train managers who were not competent in their business roles with personal computers. Jack was creating a range of training tools, such as videos and self-directed software learning programs, which he would publish for use by executives in high technology companies. Barry saw himself as a high-technology concierge who could help small companies specify, select, install and maintain the hardware and software necessary to run their businesses smoothly.

They had little or no disagreement over most decisions about the more obvious support requirements of their businesses. Bob had an investment in an office building; he suggested that space in it was available at a below market price. Even though the location seemed inconvenient, the others agreed that it met their needs. They rented the space, divided it equally and split the rental cost three ways. They shared phone service the same way. They even had consensus on style and price when they selected and purchased office furniture. They were off and running, and seemed to be able to share just about any cost between them.

About six months into the arrangement, Barry's business began to grow significantly. He asked the others if they would be willing to consider moving to a larger office location to accommodate his growth and the anticipated growth in their businesses. Although Jack was ambivalent, he was willing to go along with that choice. Without explanation, Bob said he was reluctant to move at this time, so they put off the move indefinitely.

The group had created a common account of $1,000 for office expenses. They had not set any limits, and most expenditures seemed to be small; each member of the team submitted his receipts for reimbursement regularly.

At a semi-annual review of business progress, the group agreed to have a bookkeeper handle some of the accounting chores and allow them, as principals, to spend more time promoting their businesses.

Tempers flew when they received the first expense account report. Jack was questioned about his professional publication expenses. Several of the publications and books that came in the mail were addressed to Jack, and were left for the others to read once he finished them. Since the others did not find them useful, these publications and books accumulated on the conference room table. Jack stated that he would have gotten these anyway, but believed they were relevant to the business, so he charged them to their expense account.

Barry admitted that he had charged numerous cross-country calls to the group's long distance account; he felt that it was convenient for him to do so since he did not have an account of his own, and his calls helped fill up the minimum number of long distance minutes that they were charged.

Bob's tax return was being handled by the same bookkeeper. Someone asked about the depreciation and other deductions that Bob had taken for the office building in which the group had rented space. It was a handsome deduction; Barry wanted to know if preserving this deduction was the reason he resisted making a move to new office space.

After this meeting, the group displayed minimal trust for one another; the mutual enthusiasm and support they originally had evaporated. Within six months they dissolved their incubator arrangement and went on to pursue solo business efforts.

Their naive trust in one another led to the downfall of their group enterprise. In all likelihood, each participant also damaged his ability to trust in another joint effort.

Analysis

What went wrong?

Where did Bob, Jack and Barry make their mistake?

The three business partners did not recognize each partner's need to air his requirements and expectations of the others. While the reason for working together collectively was to incubate each of their individual businesses, they overlooked the interdependence they created and the level of trust that was required.

Lessons to Be Learned

A "common property" type of relationship for the use of business resources (money, staff support, equipment, space, etc.) exposes each participant to the risk that other participants may take advantage of the situation. Abuse and exploitation can occur when the partners' needs are not discussed and the right to use common resources is not defined.

Your Turn

Answer the following questions:

► List your crucial business expenses. Check the items on the list that are also crucial for others in your business.

1.

2.

3.

4.

5.

► Do any of your joint expenses exhibit a personal gain for one partner or the other? If so, how will you balance out that gain or benefit?

► Is your venture team able to make open decisions about allocating business expenses?

See also *Getting Together: Building A Relationship That Gets To YES*, by Roger Fisher and Scott Brown, Houghton Mifflin Company, 1988.

CASE STUDY

The See-Saw of Fairness in a Business Relationship

Neglecting to balance interpersonal equities in a business relationship can undermine the success of even a professionally acclaimed business. In this case study, Betty and Jane neglected this balance for twelve years before it destroyed their public relations firm that had been among the top ten in their region.

Betty and Jane had co-owned a small public relations firm for twelve years. They started out as government employees who felt they were losing their creativity. While escaping their government roles was exhilarating, the start-up period for their new business had been difficult. In the beginning, they had shared a small office and a single telephone; it was a meager living for each of them at the start. Over the years, they had gradually built their business until it was one of the top ten public relations firms in their region.

During those twelve years, the business side of their relationship had gone fairly smoothly. Each had developed her own practice areas, and each had senior staff who could carry the work out for her.

Jane had developed an internal focus and grown her management skills for the internal tasks in the firm. Gradually, she took over control of the basic processes, such as budget development, proposal preparation, talent recruitment and strategic planning. Betty had grown to be the "external" team player. She made most of the outside contacts and was instrumental in finding most of the business for the firm.

They had also kept the personal side of their relationship compartmentalized. Betty was more socially active and spent time with her family; Jane fit the image of a highly committed professional who was consumed by the work of the firm. Only twice in the twelve years they had been in business had they found time for a "nonworking lunch." On the few occasions they and their spouses got together socially, it seemed to be very awkward for Jane.

In one particularly tense staff meeting, staff members took sides with Jane or Betty over a dispute about how to allocate the credit for landing a new piece of business. Betty and Jane decided to sort out the problem privately. Their meeting turned out to reveal the tip of an iceberg.

During that meeting, Betty and Jane both realized that their relationship was hollow. The simmering ill feelings they had for each other for twelve years emerged as an open feud. For years, Betty had resented the control that Jane had exerted on the firm's internal processes. From Betty's perspective, she was not able to do anything to please Jane. Jane resented the publicity and professional acclaim that Betty had received, believing that her own contribution was being ignored.

Attempts to get at the source of the bad feelings between them opened new wounds. Each was confounded by how the other had reacted to her own contributions to the firm. Both used the phrase "after all I've done for you and this firm, is this how you treat me?" Neither Jane nor Betty understood the animosity coming from the other.

In the months that followed that meeting, staff members made several attempts to intervene, to resolve the dispute between Betty and Jane. By this time, however, their wounds were deep and reconciliation seemed beyond hope.

The final blow to the partnership came when Betty proposed that she buy out Jane's interest in the business. This news sent the staff into a frenzy. Several senior managers departed for other firms, fearing that their positions and future professional development opportunities would be in jeopardy after a buy out.

When key clients got wind of the situation, they too re-evaluated their intention to continue working with the firm.

Analysis

What went wrong?

Where did Jane and Betty make their mistakes?

Betty and Jane did not pay attention to the missing inter-personal equity in their business relationship. Even though each thought she was "giving" in her relationship with the another, the other perceived that they were not.

In interpersonal relations, perception counts more than any-thing else. Betty and Jane perceived only what they wanted to believe about their part of the relationship—no matter what the facts said and even in the face of the other person's attempts to convince them otherwise.

Lessons to Be Learned

The scales of equity and fairness in a business relationship perform like a hidden hand, guiding and controlling the partners' contributions. You can best manage interpersonal relationships in a business setting by recognizing these factors in the perspectives you hold of others, in the expectations you have of others, in your own goal-setting, and in the feedback you offer.

Your Turn

Answer the following questions:

▶ Are you "tuned in" to what you give and what you are getting in your business relationship(s)?

▶ Do you feel overrewarded and guilty, or underrewarded and resentful?

▶ Are you or your business partner reducing your "input" to the business to compensate for something you are not getting out of the business?

See also *Managing The Equity Factor*, by Richard C. Huseman and John D. Hatfield, Houghton Mifflin Company, 1989.

CASE STUDY

When a Deal Is Not Sealed

Failing to protect the value of a business partner can have unexpected—and undesirable—results, as Larry found out in this case study.

Nick and Larry drafted a proposal for a $2 million project to produce a television series on the redevelopment of outdated factory buildings. The project was intended to be a twelve-part series for broadcast on public television network stations; it would later be repackaged as part of an educational program series for local chambers of commerce, redevelopment authorities and community groups.

They sought funds from both public and private sources. While they had not raised any formal, committed funding, they had contributed their time to the project. Larry spent the equivalent of nearly five months, full-time; Nick contributed about a month and a half, full-time.

In attempting to create an arrangement that would best suit their mix of skills and contacts, they sought to negotiate a "separate but equal" understanding that would accommodate each of their unique strengths.

Nick is a young, independent television producer with a background in urban planning and an M.A. from Harvard. He had produced a one-hour special for the Public Broadcasting System on the problems of economic development in the central provinces of Canada. The film was well received in academic circles and in "think tanks"; it became a benchmark for many stories about the redevelopment of industrial America. Nick has numerous contacts throughout the development community.

Larry is a mature, independent television producer who worked formerly with the Urban Land Institute and National Public Radio. He had produced a range of film and radio documentaries on development and redevelopment; some had been national award winners. He has experience in producing documentaries and many contacts throughout the development community, both in the public and private sectors.

Nick took the position that the production success of his Canadian feature was more valuable for generating financial support for the project, and he should have management and financial control. Larry's perspective was that he had a vision about redevelopment in industry and was able to articulate it. Larry also believed that his broad experience in many organizations would help implement the project. He did not feel that Nick had the necessary management experience, and he did not want to be managed by Nick—on this venture, or on any other.

In negotiating an agreement, Larry and Nick knew that they needed each other for the project to be successful. But they could not find a way to compose the terms and say "yes" to one another. There were many stumbling blocks to agreement. For example, since the funding sources they sought to support the project required that one person be designated as project director, how could they have a 50-50 partnership? One of them had to be accountable if they were expecting to be eligible for funding support. And, if they were both equal "owners" of this venture, would they be equally liable for actions that one of them might take regarding the project and its financial accountability?

Meanwhile, the project developed as if it had a life of its own. The momentum that had been built by Nick and Larry's initial fund-raising efforts had grown steadily. The project was on the verge of being approved in principle by the U.S. Department of Housing and Urban Development in partnership with the National Association of Manufacturers.

Nick and Larry became keenly aware that they needed to reach agreement on how the project would be managed and how they would be accountable to each other and their financial backers. It was becoming more clear all the time that this project was valuable, not only as a single project, but for its re-run and adaptation potential in local communities that have empty factory buildings that need rehabilitation.

As the time for closure on an agreement approached, Nick became more idealistic. He felt that he and Larry needed to understand each other so completely that they would think and decide as one mind. Paradoxically, while he acknowledged that he and Larry needed to submerge their egos to get the project off the ground, he still wanted to retain the "credits" as producer of the documentary.

Larry, on the other hand, only saw the agreement as a way to formalize their coordination, communication and project responsibilities. He was anxious to get the project rolling, and believed they could work out the details later. He was reluctant to see the several months of full-time effort he had invested in the project go down the drain.

After lengthy negotiations, Nick and Larry reached an understanding about how they would operate the project. They would co-sign the funding support agreements, receive equal compensation, have the exposure that each of them wanted to further their careers, and the names of their individual production companies would appear on the documentary's "credits."

About twelve months into the three-year project, Nick was killed in an accident. Their collaboration had grown much smoother than it was at the start, and Larry was saddened by the loss of his partner in this project.

Larry thought he was would be finishing the project alone, so he was flabbergasted when Nick's younger sister showed up in the production studio with an attorney and announced that she was the new partner in this documentary venture. Larry asked how could she possibly believe that she could be in this business, and she simply answered, "I inherited my brother's share of this venture. I'm his only living heir."

Analysis

What went wrong?

What mistakes did Larry make?

With most of Larry's and Nick's energies focused on getting an agreement just to get the project off the ground, Larry failed to consider the basic requirement of a buy-sell agreement: *to protect his joint investment with his business partner.*

While Nick's death was tragic and Larry found himself facing the responsibility of completing the project alone, a worse consequence was that Larry was burdened with the presence of a meddlesome heir who knew little about the project or the business, but who wanted to protect her interests.

Lessons to Be Learned

Assets of a business venture take many forms. One of the most valuable assets in a partnership is the other person; that value is intangible until he or she leaves and needs to be replaced so that the business can carry on. A simple term life insurance policy on Nick would have protected Larry from having to deal with heirs at a time when Larry needed to put all his energies into keeping the project going. Be sure to include this kind of contingency planning in your negotiations for any business partnership agreement.

Your Turn

Answer the following questions:

- ► Have you consulted an attorney about the appropriateness of using a buy-sell agreement in your business venture?

- ► Do you know how much your partner's presence would cost to replace at any point in the life of the business venture?

- ► Do you know how much your business venture is valued from year to year?

- ► What negotiation terms would be most important to you if you found you had to carry on the business alone?

See also *Deal Maker: All The Negotiating Skills And Secrets You Need,* by Robert Lawrence Kuhn, John Wiley & Sons, 1988.

CASE STUDY

Burning Business Relationship "Bridges" Before You Cross Them

If you fail to use win-win thinking to improve the terms of an existing agreement, you might be setting yourself up for disaster, as Dolores found out in this case study.

Dolores had been director of publications at a prestigious nonprofit institute. Under her direction, the institute had achieved national recognition and honors for its high-quality publications. She knew the publishing industry inside out and was well known by publishers of high-quality art books. In addition to her production experience in the publishing business, she was a respected author of several high quality "coffee table" art books.

With more than twenty years of experience in publishing, Dolores decided that she had reached the pinnacle of her position with the institute. She decided to set off on her own, to use her skills and contacts to bring authors and publishers together, and to package coffee table books for the publishing trade. To reach this goal, she created her own boutique publishing company.

Operating solo was not a practical approach in this business. She recognized that she would need the services of a graphic design firm for typesetting, composition, art work and all the production logistics that went into a high-quality art publication. Sifting through the vendors she had dealt with while she was at the institute, she settled on a small, but very competent firm headed by Bob and Oliver.

Dolores saw a synergy in working with Bob and Oliver, and proposed that they work together in a joint venture format. They agreed to terms that called for an initial start-up investment of $5000 for each of the three of them, plus $1000 each for an initial stock purchase. Dolores committed that she would give Bob and Oliver's firm all of the graphics work involved with production of the art books that she would broker and publish. (She turned out to be one of their larger clients, with design fees of about $175 thousand annually, plus administrative support and rent from a portion of their offices.)

What was not clear from their agreement was the division of labor for marketing and sales, and how efforts to bring in new business would be rewarded. Dolores worked full-time to generate proposals for new books. Her business partners contributed very little of their time to proposals and business prospecting, but were available when a new project was landed and could provide their design service for a handsome fee.

Dolores began to question the formula for sharing the work-load and profits with her venture partners. She found that her "salary" was only available on a cash-flow basis; this was a sacrifice for her since, unlike her partners, this venture was her sole source of income.

Unfortunately, her partners did not respond to her plight by making sacrifices of their own to keep the venture viable. In fact, Oliver wanted his original investment of $5000 paid off as a priority, rather than paying out any salary to Dolores.

All these factors weighed heavily on Dolores as she contemplated the fact that she was in her early 50s, had little retirement funds invested, and was working hard to sustain the business that her partners saw as a cash cow.

But she seemed stuck. Obligated to carry out several significant book projects over the next year, she had resigned herself to sticking it out, hoping that new work would produce its own rewards for her. Imagine her surprise and disappointment when she discovered in a quarterly report on the business that her partners were earning more than she was, skimming off the work she brought in.

Dolores finally faced up to the reality of her situation. She had partners who contributed the same initial capital investment as she did, but were actually drawing down a higher return because of the structure of the original agreement. She felt she was really trapped.

Analysis

What went wrong?

Where did Dolores make a mistake?

Dolores believed that conditions at the initiation of the venture would be constant over a long period of time. Therefore, she set up an agreement with her partners in the design firm without anticipating the differing levels of commitment to the business they each had. She also neglected to rebuild the relationship after she first realized that the venture was not working fairly for her.

Lessons to Be Learned

Agreements are built on relationships. While relationships often adjust to personal circumstances and business conditions, agreements tend to be seen as sacred and not to be revised.

Relationships with business partners need constant tending and reality checking. Be sure to build checkpoints into your agreements so that they can be revisited and refined as circumstances change. Dolores needed to consider scenarios like opening up new conditions in her agreement and walking away from the business. She might even have proposed to buy the existing partners out and then found alternative support services that would have met her needs.

 Your Turn

Answer the following questions:

- ► Are you able and willing to engage in a "trial relationship" for a joint venture that you are considering?

- ► Does your business agreement have opportunities for you to re-evaluate the relationship you have with your partners?

- ► Does your business agreement ensure that your income stream is protected from cash-flow fluctuations?

See also *Getting To Yes: Negotiating Agreement Without Giving In*, by Roger Fisher and William Ury, Penguin Books, 1983.

ASK YOURSELF

► What are the "ground rules" that you and your business partners want to be guided by in making your relationships?

► What type of cooperation is required for the range of decisions you and your partners make?

► How do you and your partners allocate your responsibilities in the business?

► What are your plans to re-evaluate your business agreements when an unexpected event or change occurs?

► Are yours and your partner's stake in the business still compatible?

► Is the cost of failing to address conflicts in your business relationships going unnoticed?

CHAPTER SEVEN

BENEFITING FROM THE EXPERIENCES OF OTHERS

PROFITING FROM OTHERS

Now that you have read the firsthand stories of real people like yourself who either used bad judgment or did not know better about some aspect of running their businesses, do you have a keener understanding of yourself? Are you better prepared to successfully run your own business?

By examining the mistakes of others, you have an opportunity to become better at assessing your business skills. You may have identified closely with some of the people in these case studies—perhaps not so much with the mistakes they made, but with the people and their backgrounds. You might have said to yourself, "That's me!"

The case studies in this book represent the types of people who go into small business, and what happens to them when they do. You can benefit from their experiences by avoiding the mistakes they have made.

Don't Repeat the Same Old Mistakes

As you read each of the case studies, did you see where you could have made the very same mistake? Hopefully, now that you are keenly aware of a lot of the common pitfalls of small business owners, your own experiences have been broadened vicariously. If you learned from others, you can benefit from their experiences and you will not have to learn from your own mistakes.

That Could Have Been Me

Did you sing out, "That could have been me, had I not been made aware of that type of common mistake?"

Most people who start small businesses are woefully unprepared for the undertaking. If you have wondered why so many small businesses fail, it probably became clear to you as you read that many business failures are due to ignorance.

If your standard practice is to learn from your mistakes, you will not have many chances to make mistakes in small business. The margin of error is tiny in small businesses. By learning from others, you vastly minimize your risk and enhance your chances for success.

It Is Easy to Make Mistakes

Did you learn that it does not take much to make a mistake? Some very smart people were presented in this book. They made dumb mistakes that, in many cases, destroyed their businesses.

By learning from others, you have a chance to expand your business savvy—that special sense that makes for business success. Being smart in business means being savvy—knowing the ropes and how to succeed. If you are lucky, much of this savvy can be learned from experience. In this book, you learned savvy from the experiences of others.

You Are Better Prepared

The tremendous enthusiasm and energy—and capital—that people bring to their small businesses can be sapped by the mistakes they make. By studying others, you are better prepared to look at yourself each step of the way and ask why *before* you make a mistake that could jeopardize your small business.

WHAT IS YOUR STORY?

Please share your mistake story so that others can learn and benefit. Send me your story of the mistake(s) you have made. No mistake is too small to share. Sometimes it's all the little mistakes that accumulate to impair business growth or to threaten the very existence of a small business. You will be helping other small business owners avoid common mistakes and improve their chances of success.

Use this form to detail the mistake that hurt your business. With your permission, we'll share your story in the next volume of *Avoiding Mistakes In Your Small Business*. We will not use your real name, so please be totally honest.

HERE IS MY STORY:

▶ Describe your small business.

▶ Discuss your reason(s) for starting your business.

▶ What is your formal educational background?

▶ Describe your small business background.

▶ Describe, in detail, the mistake you made that is worth sharing.

▶ How badly did the mistake you made hurt your business?

▶ How could you have avoided your mistake?

▶ Do we have your permission to use your story, provided we change the names?

_____

Please print your name

_____   _____

Your signature   *Date*

Thank you on behalf of all those who will benefit from your experience. Please mail this form to:

Dr. David Karlson
8004 Ellingson Drive
Chevy Chase, MD 20815

APPENDIX

WORKSHEETS FOR BUSINESS RELATIONSHIPS
[With Questions Designed To Reveal Each Owner's Concerns And Interests]
by Tom Mierzwa, 1992

I. UNDERSTANDINGS YOU HAVE WITH BUSINESS PARTNERS

A. Personal Intentions:

What is your **primary personal reason** for forming this enterprise?

_____
_____
_____
_____

What are your **secondary reasons**?

_____
_____
_____
_____

B. Business Intention:

What is the **purpose and mission** of this business enterprise?

_____
_____
_____
_____

C. Acknowledgements:

What **strengths** do you bring to this business relationship?

_____
_____
_____
_____

What are your **weaknesses**?

_____
_____
_____
_____

What strengths do your business **partners** bring to this relationship?

_____
_____
_____
_____

What are their weaknesses?

_____
_____
_____
_____

D. Risks:

What **personal risks** are at stake for you in this business relationship?

_____
_____
_____
_____

What **professional risks** are at stake?

_____
_____
_____
_____

II. OWNERSHIP CONTRIBUTIONS

A. To Date:

What have been your **monetary** contributions?

_____
_____
_____
_____

What **in-kind** contributions have you made?

_____
_____
_____
_____

B. Future:

Under what **conditions** would you make (further) monetary contributions to this enterprise?

_____
_____
_____
_____

III. COMPENSATION

A. Salary/Fee:

In what ways must **salary/fee levels** meet your current needs?

_____
_____
_____
_____

What are your **future expectations**. . . . in 1 yr . . . 3 yrs . . . 5yrs?

_____
_____
_____
_____

B. Incentives:

What incentive/bonus arrangements should match your **performance** in this business?

_____
_____
_____
_____

C. Owner Equity:

What **share** of equity in this enterprise is allocated for each owner?

_____
_____
_____
_____

What are your **future expectations** for allocating equity in this enterprise?

_____

_____

_____

_____

IV. OPERATION OF THE BUSINESS

A. Management Roles:

For each major area of the business, which are you **most interested** in taking responsibility for?

_____

_____

_____

_____

Which areas are you **least interested** in?

_____

_____

_____

_____

Are there roles which you do **not** want responsibility for?

_____

_____

_____

_____

B. Decision-Making:

For major areas of the business, by what **method** would you want to reach key decisions or commitments in each of those areas? (Jointly? By Consensus? Collaboratively? By Designating Accountability? . . . Or by other methods?)

_____
_____
_____
_____

C. Expenses:

What are your expectations about reasonable expenses and how much **discretion** should be allowed in spending by business partners?

_____
_____
_____
_____

D. Time Commitment:

What expectations do you have **for yourself** regarding time committed to a "work day"?

_____
_____
_____
_____

What are your expectations of time commitment **by your partners**?

_____
_____
_____
_____

What expectations do you have for yourself regarding vacation time and personal time away from the business?

_____

_____

_____

_____

What are your expectations about personal time for your partners?

_____

_____

_____

_____

V. GROWING THE BUSINESS

A. New Business Areas:

What are your expectations regarding the types of **product/service offerings** this enterprise might offer in the future?

_____

_____

_____

_____

What about expansion into new geographic market areas?

_____

_____

_____

_____

B. Additional Owners:

What **expectations and qualifications** for additional business partners would meet your interests?

_____

_____

_____

_____

VI. ENDING THE BUSINESS

A. Involuntarily:

What are your **expectations** for the business in the event of death or disability of a partner?

_____

_____

_____

_____

B. Voluntarily:

What are your **expectations** for the business if a partner decided to leave or retire from the business?

_____

_____

_____

_____

What **conditions** would protect your interests in this enterprise in the event of a departing partner?

_____

_____

_____

_____

VII. UPDATING THESE START-UP GROUND RULES

A. Scope:

What are the types of conditions or circumstances under which you would like to have these ground rules updated?

_____
_____
_____
_____

B. Periodic Review:

How frequently would you like to have a review of how these ground rules are working with your business partners?

_____
_____
_____

RESOURCES

ADDITIONAL SOURCES

No single book, person, government document, agency or organization has all the answers you will need to start your business. Consequently, you should consult a variety of sources after you read this book. First, contact your local library and your nearby Small Business Administration office (addresses for S.B.A. regional and district offices are included below). These two sources will give you the most *bang for your buck.*

If your local library has been designated as a *government depository* most of the census data and other government documents, statistics, reports, etc. you will need will be available.

The S.B.A. will be able to answer your specific questions about operating a business in your state. They will be able to refer you to the right agencies for information pertaining to any licenses or permits you may need. They will also be able to provide you with a wealth of small business bibliographies, booklets and pamphlets covering a wide range of relevant topics. Ask for their list of "Business Development Booklets, Form 115B," and their list of "Business Development Pamphlets, Form 115A." They may also be able to recommend new-business workshops held in your area.

Here are some additional specific sources of information you might wish to investigate:

S.B.A. Regional Offices

60 Batterymarch Street, 10th Floor
Boston, MA 02110
(617) 223-3204

26 Federal Plaza, Room 29-118
New York, NY 10278
(212) 264-7772

231 Saint Asaphs Road, #640
Bala Cnywyd, PA 19004
(215) 596-5889

1375 Peachtree Street, N.E.
Atlanta, GA 30367
(404) 881-4999

219 South Dearborn Street, #838
Chicago, IL 60604
(312) 353-0359

S.B.A District Offices

150 Causeway Street, 10th Floor
Boston, MA 02114
(617) 223-3224

40 Western Avenue, #512
Augusta, ME 04330
(207) 622-8378

55 Pleasant Street, #211
Concord, NH 03301
(603) 224-4041

One Hartford Square West
Hartford, CT 06106
(203) 244-3600

87 State Street, #205
Montpelier, VT 05602
(802) 229-0538

40 Fountain Street
Providence, RI 02903
(401) 528-4580

Carlos Chardon Avenue, #691
Hato Rey, PR 00919
(809) 753-4002

970 Broad Street, #1635
Newark, NJ 07102
(201) 645-2434

100 South Clinton Street, #1071
Syracuse, NY 13260
(315) 423-5383

8600 LaSalle Road, #630
Towson, MD 21204
(301) 962-4392

109 North 3rd Street, #320
Clarksburg, WV 26301
(304) 623-5631

960 Penn Avenue, 5th Floor
Pittsburgh, PA 15222
(412) 644-2780

400 North 8th Street, #3015
Richmond, VA 23240
(804) 771-2617

1111 18th Street, N.W., 6th Floor
Washington, D.C. 20417
(202) 634-4950

1720 Peachtree Road, N.W., 7th Floor
Atlanta, GA 30309
(404) 881-4749

908 South 20th Street, #200
Birmingham, AL 35256
(205) 254-1344

230 S. Tryon Street, #700
Charlotte, NC 28202
(704) 371-6563

1835 Assembly Street, 3rd Floor
Columbia, SC 29201
(803) 765-5376

100 West Capitol Street, #322
Jackson, MS 39269
(601) 960-4378

400 West Bay Street, #261
Jacksonville, FL 32202
(904) 791-3782

600 Federal Place, #188
Louisville, KY 40202
(502) 582-5971

2222 Ponce de Leon Blvd., 5th Floor
Miami, FL 33134
(305) 350-5521

404 James Robertson Parkway, #1012
Nashville, TN 37219
(615) 251-5881

1240 East 9th Street, #317
Cleveland, OH 44199
(216) 522-4170

85 Marconi Blvd.
Columbus, OH 43215
(614) 469-6860

477 Michigan Avenue, #515
Detroit, MI 18006
(313) 226-7241

595 N. Pennsylvania Street, #578
Indianapolis, IN 46209
(317) 269-7272

212 East Washington Avenue, #213
Madison, WI 53703
(608) 264-5261

100 North 6th Street
Minneapolis, MN 55403
(612) 349-3550

Government Publications

U. S. Treasury Department
Internal Revenue Service
Washington, D.C. 20224

- ▶ Tax Guide for Small Business (Publication #334)

- ▶ Tax Guide on Depreciation (Publication #534)

- ▶ Employer's Tax Guide (Publication 15, circular E)

- ▶ Information Returns (Publication #916)

- ▶ Tax Calendar and Check List (Publication #509)

The Superintendent of Documents
U. S. Government Printing Office
Washington, D. C. 20402
(202) 783-3238

- ▶ Franchise Opportunities Handbook

- ▶ Census Catalog and Guide (published annually)

- ▶ Standards for General Industry (O.S.H.A. guidelines)

- ▶ U. S. Government Purchasing and Sales Directory

Useful Indices Commonly Found In Libraries

Standard Industrial Classification Manual
Guide that provides unique number, i.e., SIC code, for each
industry. Many other data sources are organized by SIC codes.)

Business Periodicals Index
Index to information found in business periodicals and journals.

Predicasts Funk and Scott Index of Corporations and Industries
Index to information about goods, services, specific companies
and industries found in business periodicals and journals.

American Statistics Index (A.S.I): A Comprehensive Guide and Index to the Statistical Publications of the U. S. Government
Very comprehensive source includes abstracts.

Other Useful Library Sources

Statistical Abstract of the United States
Contains brief statistical summaries from governmental and nongovernmental sources. Useful in preliminary stages of market or industry analyses.

County and City Data Book
Includes useful market statistics for cities, counties, and states in the U. S.

"State" Statistical Abstract
Separate volume published for each state, covers seventeen categories of statistics within the state: e.g., employement and earnings, banking and finance, crime and public safety, vital statistics.

Survey of Buying Power
Special issue of *Sales and Marketing Management* containing statistical data for cities, counties, and metropolitan areas in the U. S. Popular Buying Power Index is also included for each area.

Census of Retail Trade
Several census publications providing retail trade statistics for a number of industries and geographic areas.

Standard and Poors Register
Provides useful data and descriptions of industries in the U.S., arranged by SIC fode.

Annual Statement Studies, by Robert Morris Associates
Useful financial ratio data for several types of businesses.

Directories

Business Capital Sources
International Wealth Success
24 Canterbury Road
Rockville Center, NY 11570

Canadian Trade Directory, Fraser's
481 University Avenue
Toronto, Ontario
Canada M5W1A4

Co-ops, Voluntary Chains and Wholesale Grocers
425 Park Avenue
New York, NY 10022

Credit and Sales Reference Directory
222 Cedar Lane
Teaneck NJ 07666

Department Stores
425 Park Avenue
New York, NY 10022

Direct Selling Companies/A Supplier's Guide
1730 M Street, NW
Washington, DC 20036

Distribution Services Guide
Chilton Way
Radnor, PA 19089

Dun & Bradstreet Middle Market Directory
99 Church Street
New York, NY 10007

Dun & Bradstreet Million Dollar Directory
99 Church Street
New York, NY 10007

Food Brokers' Association, National Directory of Members
1916 M Street, NW
Washington, DC 20036

Food Service Distributors
425 Park Avenue
New York, NY 10022

General Merchandise, Variety and Junior Department Stores
425 Park Avenue
New York, NY 10022

Thomas' Grocery Register
One Penn Plaza
New York, NY 10001

Mailing List Houses Directory
P.O. Box 8503
Coral Springs, FL 33065

Major Mass Market Merchandisers
1140 Broadway
New York, NY 10001

Manufacturers & Agents National Association Directory of
Members
P.O. Box 16878
Irvine, CA 92713

Manufacturers' Representatives Directory
135 Addison Avenue
Elmhurst, IL 60126

Mail Order Business Directory
P.O. Box 8503
Coral Springs, FL 33065

Mass Retailing Merchandisers Buyers' Directory
222 West Avenue
Chicago, IL 60606

National Buyers' Guide 1980
115 Second Avenue
Waltham, MA 02154

National Mailing-List Houses
P.O. Box 15434
Ft. Worth, TX 76119

National Wholesale Druggists' Association Membership and Executive Directory
670 White Plains Road
Scarsdale, NY 10583

Non-Food Buyers National Directory
1372 Peachtree Street, NE
Atlanta, GA 30309

Sources of Supply Buyers' Guide
P.O. Drawer 795
Park Ridge, IL 60068

Supermarket, Grocery & Convenience Store Chains
425 Park Avenue
New York, NY 10022

U. S. Government Purchasing and Sales Directory
U. S. Government Printing Office
Washington, DC 20402

Wholesalers and Manufacturers Directory
1514 Elmwood Avenue
Evanston, IL 60201

Trade and Professional Associations

American Entrepreneurs' Association
2311 Pontius Avenue
Los Angeles, CA 90064

American Federation of Small Business
407 South Dearborn Street
Chicago, IL 60605

American Management Association
135 West 50th Street
New York, NY 10020

American Marketing Association
250 South Wacker Drive
Chicago, IL 60606

American Retail Federation
1616 H Street, NW
Washington, DC 20006

National Association of Retail Grocers of United States
P.O. Box 17208
Washington, DC 20041

National Association of Variety Stores
7646 West Devon Avenue
Chicago, IL 60631

National Consumer Finance Association
1000 Sixteenth Street, NW
Washington, DC 20036

National Federation of Independent Business
150 W. 20th Avenue
San Mateo, CA 94403

National Small Business Association
1604 K Street, N.W.
Washington, DC 20006

Small Business Foundation of America
20 Park Plaza
Boston, MA 02116

Smaller Manufacturers Council
339 Blvd. of the Allies
Pittsburgh, PA 15322

Periodicals

American Journal of Small Business
University of Baltimore, School of Business
Baltimore, MD 21201

Business Today
P.O. Box 10010
1720 Washington Blvd.
Ogden, UT 84409

Entrepreneur Magazine
2311 Pontius Avenue
Los Angeles, CA 90064

Dynamic Business
Smaller Manufacturers Council
339 Blvd. of the Allies
Pittsburgh, PA 15222

In Business: For the Independent, Innovative Individual
J.G. Press
P.O. Box 351
Emmaus, PA 18049

Inc., The Magazine for Growing Companies
38 Commercial Wharf
Boston, MA 02110

Income Opportunities
380 Lexington Avenue
New York, NY 10017

Journal of Business Venturing
Elsevier Science Publishing Company, Inc.
P.O. Box 1663, Grand Central Station
New York, NY 10163

Bureau of Business Research
P.O. Box 6025
Morgantown, WV 26506

Manage
2210 Arbor Boulevard
Dayton, OH 45439

New Business
P.O. Box 3312
Sarasota, FL 33578

Opportunity Magazine
6 N. Michigan Ave., Suite 1405
Chicago, IL 60602

S.A.M. Advanced Management Journal
Society for the Advancement of Management
135 West 50th
New York, NY 10020

Small Business Report
203 Calle Del Oaks
Monterey, CA 93940

Success Magazine
342 Madison Avenue
New York, NY 10173

Venture Magazine, Inc.
521 5th Avenue
New York, NY 10175

Books

Accounting Principles, by C. R. Niswonger and P. E. Fess
South-Western Publishing Company
Cincinnati, OH

Beacham's Marketing References, Walton Beacham, Richard T. Hise,
and Hale N. Tongren, eds., 1986
Research Publishing
Washington, D.C.
(Small business focus with annotated bibliographies for each
marketing topic)

Creating the Successful Business Plan For New Ventures, by LaRue
Hosmer and Roger Guiles
McGraw-Hill Book Company
P.O. Box 400
Hightstown, NJ 08520-9989

Effective Small Business Management, 2nd ed., by N. M.
Scarborough and T. W. Zimmerer, 1988
Merrill Publishing Company
Columbus, OH 43216

Encyclopedia of Business Information Sources, 6th edition, 1987 by
Paul Wasserman, et al
Gale Research Company, Book Tower
Detroit, MI 48226

The Encyclopedia of Management, Carl Heyel, editor
Van Nostrand Reinhold Co.
450 W. 33rd Street
New York, NY 10001

Entrepreneurship: Creativity at Work
Harvard Business Review
P.O. Box 866
Farmingdale, NY 11737-9966

Essentials of Managerial Finance, by J. F. Weston and E. F. Brigham
The Dryden Press
Hinsdale, IL

Fundamentals of Marketing, 8th ed., by W. J. Stanton and Charles
Futrell, 1987
McGraw-Hill Book Company
New York, NY

Guide to Consumer Markets
The Conference Board
845 Third Avenue
New York, NY 10022
(Updated every 2 years)

The Guide to Understanding Financial Statements, by S. B. Costales
McGraw-Hill Book Company
P.O. Box 400
Hightstown, NJ 08520-9989

How to Incorporate: A Handbook for Entrepreneurs and Professionals,
by M. R. Diamond and J. L. Williams, 1987
John Wiley and Sons, Inc.
P.O. Box 6793
Somerset, NJ 08873-9977

How to Really Manage Inventories, by Hal Mather
McGraw-Hill Book Company
P.O. Box 400
Hightstown, NJ 08520-9989

How to Run a Small Business, by J. K. Lasser Tax Institute
McGraw-Hill Book Company
P.O. Box 400
Hightstown, NJ 08520-9989

Information Bank for Entrepreneurs
American Entrepreneurs Association
2311 Pontius Avenue
Los Angeles, CA 90064

Modern Retailing: Theory and Practice, by J. B. Mason and M. L. Mayer
Business Publications, Inc.
Plano, TX 75075

Planning and Financing Your New Business: A Guide to Venture Capital
Technology Management
57 Kilvert Street
Warwick, RI 02886

Purchase and Sale of Small Businesses: Tax and Legal Aspects, by M. J. Lane
John Wiley and Sons, Inc.
605 3rd Avenue
New York, NY 10158

The Selection Of Retail Locations, Richard L. Nelson, 1958
F. W. Dodge Corporation
New York, NY
(a classic)

The Small Business Index, by Wayne D. Kryszak
Scarecrow Press, Inc.
52 Liberty Street
Metuchen, NJ 08840
(a bibliography)

Small Business Information Sources: An Annotated Bibliography, by
Joseph C. Schabacker, 1976
National Council for Small Business Management Develop-
ment—University of Wisconsin Extension
929 North Sixth Street
Milwaukee, WI 53203

The Small Business Legal Advisor, by William A. Hancock
McGraw-Hill Book Company
P.O. Box 400
Hightstown, NJ 08520-9989

*Small Business: Look Before You Leap; A Catalogue of Sources of
Information To Help You Start and Manage Your Own Small Business,*
Louis Mucciolo, editor
Arco Publishing Company
215 Park Avenue South
New York, NY 10003

Small Business Sourcebook, and Urban Business Profiles
Gale Research Company
Book Tower
Detroit, MI 48226

Strategic Planning for Smaller Businesses, by David A. Curtis, 1983
Lexington Books (D.C. Health and Company)
Lexington, MA

Who's Who In Venture Capital, by A. David Silver
John Wiley and Sons, Inc.
P.O. Box 6793
Somerset, NJ 08873-9977

Miscellaneous Services

Bureau of Business Research
200 CBA
The University of Nebraska
Lincoln, NE 68588-0409
location research

Nielson Business Services
A. C. Nielson Company
Nielson Plaza
Northbrook, IL 60062
commercial market research

Reid Psychological Systems
233 North Michigan Avenue
Chicago, IL 60601
paper and pencil honesty exams

Venture Capital Network, Inc.
P.O. Box 882
Durham, NH 03824
non-profit service to match entrepreneurs with potential individual investors

Yankelovich Skelly and White
575 Madison Avenue
New York, NY 10022
commercial market research

ABOUT THE AUTHOR

For eight years, Dr. David Karlson has been a consultant to small business principals. He is the author of *Marketing Your Consulting or Professional Services* (Crisp Publications, 1988), which has helped thousands of professionals expand their marketing skills to sell their services effectively. He also wrote *Consulting for Success: A Practical Guide for Prospective Consultants* (Crisp Publications, 1991), which has been a guidebook for thousands of individuals who have considered entering the consulting field.

Dr. Karlson is currently planning the next volume of *Avoiding Mistakes in Your Small Business*. He welcomes your comments and encourages you to use the form in this book to send him your "mistake story" so that others can learn and benefit from your experience.

ABOUT THE CONTRIBUTING AUTHOR

For twelve years, Tom Mierzwa has been a consultant to small businesses on company formation, strategic planning, and operational harmony. His approach for fashioning working agreements uses the mediation process supported with creative problem-solving tools.

NOTES

NOTES

NOTES

ABOUT CRISP PUBLICATIONS

We hope that you enjoyed this book. If so, we have good news for you. This title is only one in the library of Crisp's best-selling books. Each of our books is easy to use and is obtainable at a very reasonable price.

Books are available from your distributor. A free catalog is available upon request from Crisp Publications, Inc., 1200 Hamilton Court, Menlo Park, California 94025. Phone: (415) 323-6100; Fax: (415) 323-5800.

Books are organized by general subject area.

Computer Series

Management Training

Personal Improvement

Communications

Small Business and Financial Planning